D1571856

Riding Time Like a River

Riding Time Like A River

The Catholic Moral Tradition Since Vatican II

EDITED BY
William J. O'Brien

GEORGETOWN UNIVERSITY PRESS / WASHINGTON, D.C.

Georgetown University Press, Washington, D.C.   20057–1079
© 1993 by Georgetown University Press. All rights reserved.
Printed in the United States of America
10 9 8 7 6 5 4 3 2 1   1993
THIS VOLUME IS PRINTED ON ACID-FREE OFFSET BOOK PAPER.

Library of Congress Cataloging-in-Publication Data

Riding time like a river : the Catholic moral tradition since Vatican
   II / edited by William J. O'Brien
        p.   cm.
     1. Christian ethics--Catholic authors.   2. Catholic Church-
   -Doctrines.   I. O'Brien, William James.
   BJ1249.R53   1993   241'.042'09045--dc20   93-4394
   ISBN 0-87840-542-9

Contents

Introduction

The Second Vatican Council, which took place in Rome between December 1963 and January 1965, is of epochal significance for Roman Catholics. Its ringing *aggiornamento* reverberated throughout the Catholic world, promising a profound renewal at every level of church life. A church known for its monolithic unity, symbolized for many by the Latin mass at the universal center of its ritual life, in an outburst of pentecostal enthusiasm suddenly began to speak in tongues that men and women of all nations could, with effort, understand. An entire generation has grown to maturity in the years following Vatican II, years largely spent assimilating the fruits of its labors.

The years of assimilation have not been without moments of dismay for those who have been caught up in the drama. The old *extra ecclesiam, nulla salus* gave way to an interest in ecumenical dialogue both among Christians of different confessions and between Christians and members of other religious traditions, and questions of a pluralism within Christian faith emerged with increasing frequency.

The Council's decrees and determinations also carried implications for an understanding of the Catholic moral tradition. That tradition had always been understood to comprise a number of essential elements: biblical, historical, philosophical, and scientific. But the winds that blew through the Council chambers stirred each of those elements profoundly. The Council's blessing on modern historical-critical methods in the study of biblical sources, for example, revolutionized the study of scripture in Catholic circles. Texts once regarded as eye witness reports about Jesus of Nazareth are now seen as expressions of the faith of Christians living generations after the events described in the biblical narratives. Texts once regarded as objective grounds for moral arguments are now understood within historical and cultural contexts that may or may not have a bearing on questions and issues arising in later, quite different historical and cultural contexts. The ground on which one used to imagine oneself standing began to move. One begins to feel more like someone riding a river, riding time like a river.

The image need not be unsettling. Like a river, the Catholic moral tradition springs from a source at once mysterious and divine. It courses down the centuries through many lands on its journey to the sea, nourishing those who draw from its living waters. Six essays on the Catholic moral tradition collected in this volume were initially presented as lectures on the campus of Georgetown University early in 1992. The theme for the series and the title for the book, "Riding Time Like A River," was adapted from a line in Gerard Manley Hopkins's *Wreck of the Deutschland* and speaks to the dynamism of that tradition.

In the opening essay, Leo J. O'Donovan, S.J., president of Georgetown University, artfully renders the lay of the land for those who would ride the river. He asks how one is to understand the authority of Christ and the authority of culture in institutions of Catholic learning. H. Richard Niebuhr's classic *Christ and Culture* and the more recent writing of Avery Dulles,S.J., provide the frames for his original sketch, from which issue seven guidelines for those who would negotiate the currents:

1. Be comprehensive in grasping the dialogue of Christ and culture and be aware of its complexity.
2. Beware of understanding the gospel and the church as primarily "countercultural."
3. Beware of "cultural enthusiasm."
4. Avoid reducing the dialogue between gospel and culture to a single issue.
5. Learn from the church's historical breadth.
6. Understand that politics and prayer, mysticism and worldliness are inseparable moments in the dialogue.
7. Reserve the final judgment to God.

These guidelines enable those who would embark on the journey to take their bearings.

Richard A. McCormick, S.J., whose *Notes on Moral Theology* in the decades following Vatican II kept American Catholic moral theologians on track, sets out to reimagine his discipline as he hopes it will appear in the year 2000. To reimagine in this way, he suggests, is to dream: "to foresee options and possibilities in order to burst the bonds of conventionality, and allow Christianity not only to remember the past but to create the future and thereby to meet the theological and pastoral needs of the believing community."

Such a moral theology, he suggests, will be christocentric, with charity as its heart and soul; universal in its appeal and applicability rather than sectarian; characterized by a principle of subsidiarity according to which lay persons have distinctive roles according to their competence; personalist (that is, attentive to all facets and dimensions of the human person rather than to a single, isolated function like the biological); modest and tentative; truly ecumenical; inductive in method; tolerant of pluralism; aspirational; and specialistic rather than omnicompetent. Such distinctions enable those on board to set their course.

John Noonan's years in the judiciary as well as his patient historical research contribute to his profound appreciation for past human achievements in law and in morality. He is like an oarsman who searches out the deep and mighty currents in favor of eddies that divert one from the journey. He focuses his attention on the language of morals and, in particular, on three foundational metaphors: nature, reciprocity, and the last judgment. As metaphors, they must be "narrowly watched," because they have an almost hypnotic power to shape developments in ways that defy reason. At the same time, he concludes, "none of these metaphors would have worked at all if it had been completely arbitrary, if there had not been a response in human experience, if it were not true that human beings do have purposes that are not entirely malleable; that there is a rhythm in human interaction that produces equivalences, that, in some sense, to someone—ourselves or another—we are accountable, and that that accountability holds promise." In short, these foundational metaphors within the Catholic moral tradition point to universal human characteristics that make moral discourse possible and profitable. In this regard, Noonan and McCormick agree that the Catholic moral tradition is anything but sectarian.

Louis Dupré identifies and traces not the foundational metaphors of morals but fundamental philosophies that the Catholic moral tradition has incorporated from its earliest days. As holder of the Catholic chair in the philosophy of religion at Yale University, Dupré is well positioned to reflect on the relation of philosophy and theology, religion and culture. On the one hand, he can agree with Karl Jaspers that the absoluteness of the moral imperative need not imply the existence of God, that the atheist is as capable of morality as the believer. On the other, he can and does show that the Catholic moral tradition has always been "aspirational" in the sense advocated by McCormick. Citing Francis of Assisi and Mother Theresa as examples, he observes that "what began as the gratuitous action of a single individual becomes incorporated into our moral *patrimonium* and the exception becomes part of the common ideal." Ironically, such individuals who seem not particularly concerned about morality are capable of transforming it. Their actions, "in some respects questionable and in all respects 'useless,'" are transformed "into symbols of a higher moral demand."

New Testament scholar John Donahue, S.J., calls attention to the problem that arises when one distinguishes between a heroic Christian morality based on the example of Jesus and a morality of ordinary Christians based, more often than not, on an understanding of the natural law: namely, the neglect of the prophetic challenge of the New Testament in Roman Catholic moral theology. In this light, the Second Vatican Council's blessing of historical criticism in biblical study was revolutionary. Donahue isolates seven major contributions of New Testament study to moral theology and, by implication, to the continued development of the Catholic moral tradition:

1. Consensus among exegetes that New Testament ethics in the technical sense of a systematic treatise on the principles and practice of Christian life does not exist. By implication, Christian ethics cannot be reduced to New Testament teaching.
2. Refusal to study ethics in isolation from other theological disciplines that center on the Christ event and on an understanding of communal life in Christ.
3. Dissolution of the distinction between a heroic ethics modeled on saintly lives and an ethics cut to the measure of the ordinary Christian. When Paul urges the church at Philippi to "look not to your own interests but to the interest of others," he presents the death of Christ as a model for Christians in the conduct of their ordinary lives.
4. Realization that ethical pluralism has existed in Christianity from the very beginning.
5. Realization of the need to take into account a variety of sources of authority and reflection, including scriptural texts, the community's tradition of faith and practice, as well as normative and descriptive accounts of human life.
6. Realization that the dialogue between the Bible and Christian ethics must become communal and pastoral in both method and content. Not "What should I do?" but "What should we do?" is the primary question to bring to a very collaborative effort.
7. Realization that ethical issues emerge in particular historical contexts, often in response to definite historical situations.

John Mahoney, S.J., whose recent book, *The Making of Moral Theology*, is fast becoming a standard text for moral theologians, reiterates

Dupré's suggestion that an ethical tradition of conscience is strengthened by the religious tradition of discernment and builds on Donahue's position by suggesting that it is finally fulfilled in the theological (that is, biblical) tradition of prophecy.

He begins by tracing a broad outline of the classical tradition of conscience from Paul through the early church fathers and medieval scholastics to the Second Vatican Council. He then notes that moral decision making can be viewed in a religious context within which the central question is not the ethical question, "What ought I to do?" but the religious question, "What is God calling or inviting me to do?" The Catholic tradition of spirituality has much to offer one disposed to raise this question. Not incidentally, the role of the religious community has grown in significance as a check on any individual's claim to be carrying out God's will.

Mahoney devotes the final pages of his essay to a reflection on the way in which moral theology should be moving. If the classical tradition of conscience is the mainstream, and if the religious tradition of discernment is a placid tributary, a powerful hidden stream yet to tap is the theological tradition of prophecy: "What is now under consideration is not just authenticating what one considers is God's influence on the heart of the individual as she or he considers moral decisions. What is now at stake is scrutinizing and validating the witness that God is calling one to offer to the church and the larger community."

When all is said and done, however, how one acts in conscience—how one rides the river—remains the central issue. Sidney Callahan concludes this set of essays with a synopsis of her recent monograph on this subject. She begins by examining conscience not as any kind of thing or object but as a complex human activity. She defines conscience as "a personal, self-conscious activity that integrates reason, intuition, emotion, and will in self-committed decisions about right and wrong, good and evil." Moreover, she sees the activity of conscience as "recursive, oscillating, interactive [and] dynamic" rather than as "orderly, linear, rationalistic." Reason, intuition, and emotions "mutually influence each other in the complex decision making of conscience."

Although the role of reason in moral decision making has received centuries of attention, the role of intuition has been less noted. Though Callahan places considerable emphasis on the importance of intuitions for the moral life, she insists that they be rationally tested and grounded.

If intuition has been widely ignored, emotions have been actively distrusted by those who have examined moral decision making. Callahan notes the recent explosion of research on emotion in psychology and suggests that emotions play an essential role in the moral life and, like intuitions, can be valuable resources for the person who desires to act morally.

In sum, "reason judges feeling, feelings and intuitions assess reasoning. Spontaneous or enacted emotions tutor emotions. We may wait upon intuitions or seek an intuitive sense of rightness and appropriateness in our arguments and feelings. All our capacities, dimensions, or subselves are plumbed and engaged in coming to a personal, wholehearted moral commitment." One so engaged finds it only natural to "seek information, guidance, and consultation with the wise and good and within [one's] traditional community." As each of the contributors to this volume has demonstrated, no one rides the river alone.

WILLIAM J. O'BRIEN

1

Christ, Culture, and the Foundations of Authority

Most Christians are familiar with the grandeur of the Great Commission that concludes the Gospel of St. Matthew. Sited on the Mount of Revelation, it summarizes the authority of the kingdom of God that has been bestowed on Jesus, his missionary command to teach all peoples the good news, and the assurance of his divine presence, Emmanuel with his people, for all time. The text reads:

> Now the eleven disciples went to Galilee, to the mountain to which Jesus had directed them. And when they saw him they worshiped him; but some doubted. And Jesus came and said to them, "All authority in heaven and on earth has been given to me. Go therefore and make disciples of all nations, baptizing them in the name of the Father and of the Son and of the Holy Spirit, teaching them to observe all that I have commanded you; and lo, I am with you always, to the close of the age" (Matt 28:16-20).

The passage is both exalted and comforting, as human as it is demanding, as universal as it is challenging. The disciples worship Jesus, yet there is room for human doubt. They hear his claim to absolute authority, but in the human form they have touched and talked to. They are to lead all men and women toward union with the transcendent God, but it will be the God of a suffering Jesus, and through his compassionate Spirit. They are to teach all he has taught them, in fulfillment of the Hebrew Scripture. And he will be with them, personally and always, as they baptize and teach, pray and preach, reflect and act. All authority is his.

AUTHORITY AND EPOCHAL CHANGE

The claim seems clear enough, and urgently appropriate, at a time of such fundamental transformations as we are now experiencing

1

throughout the world. I need not detail the economic, political, and cultural changes that have rushed upon us over the past several years. Since the revolution of freedom in Eastern Europe, momentarily overshadowed in the winter of 1990–1991 by the crisis in the Persian Gulf, and now recast in terms of the dissolution of the U.S.S.R., we realize that we are living through one of the great watersheds in world history.

Catholic higher education also finds itself at a crossroads that may be described as critical—and for several reasons. First, in the wake of the Second Vatican Council, the Catholic church continues to pursue an epochal renewal. For a decade or so after the Council, many of us had hoped that the renewal of the church could be effected before our very eyes. Now we see that a worldwide *aggiornamento* of the church requires greater labor, greater sacrifice, greater wisdom than we could appreciate some years ago. It also involves new relations with other Christian churches, with Judaism, with other world religions. Above all, the situation of the church in the world is more complex, dynamic, and ambiguous than our theology to date has been able to conceptualize. As Karl Rahner insisted, we are only beginning to realize the implications of the Spirit's call to be a church in the whole world.[1]

Second, in recent decades the Catholic church in the United States has experienced enormous growth and very significant prosperity. We are no longer a church that is defensive in regard to the mainstream of American society; in most respects we have entered that mainstream. At the same time, a new wave of immigrants from Southeast Asia and Latin America is significantly changing the complexion of the church for the future.[2]

Third, the relationship between the Catholic community and the nation at large has shifted. Catholic universities will have new responsibilities in a nation where Catholics are called to share leadership in every area of the nation's life. At such a time it will be all the more important for them to develop as true universities, maintaining a genuine commitment to creative teaching but also making real contributions to the advance of learning through research. They must also, of course, pay continuing and serious attention to their identity as Catholic institutions. I quote frequently an editorial in *America* magazine that speaks of Catholic higher education in our nation as an achievement comparable to the work of the Benedictine monasteries in the seventh century or the founding of the medieval universities in the Middle Ages.[3] Now, in concert with other churches in America, Catholicism is awakening to the need for a more critical and reflective contribution to the pluralistic society from which it has benefited so much.

There are many aspects of Catholic higher education which should be addressed from a specifically educational point of view. We need to be as clear as possible, for example, about the identity and mission of Catholic educational institutions. Pope John Paul II's *Ex Corde Ecclesiae*, the Apostolic Constitution on Catholic Universities, marks a major stage in the history of church teaching and reflection on the subject. In at least two important respects, the papal document incorporates significant improvements over earlier drafts. First, it recognizes that universities vary significantly from one part of the world to another and that the cultural differences of the societies in which they develop must be respected if the institutions are to succeed. Second, the final document recognizes that the primary responsibility for the Catholic character of the institution lies with the institution itself. But further interpretation and reception will be necessary for the full import of the Constitution to appear.[4]

A further area of concern will be theology's place in Catholic higher education. The case of Father Charles Curran and the troubling implications it raises for academic freedom remain with us. The revised Profession of Faith and new Oath of Loyalty promulgated by the Congregation for the Doctrine of Faith in 1989 still raise unsettled questions.[5] The 1990 instruction on the ecclesial vocation of the theologian has also been variously interpreted.[6] While it has had many critics, some very astute commentators, including Archbishop John Quinn and Father Avery Dulles, consider it an advance.

Third, moral teaching in particular will receive increased attention in the years to come. Whether further Roman documents address the subject or not, continued tension is likely not only about particular moral issues but especially about the methodology of the field itself.[7]

Fourth, American Catholic universities will be under increasing financial strain, as will all higher education in the United States. Father Edward Malloy of Notre Dame has argued that universities, in consequence, will need to state their vision even more clearly and be more participative in attracting the help of their friends than they have been in the past.[8]

These aspects of Catholic education could be discussed at some length. But I would like to probe a deeper issue, one that underlies everything else that is pursued in a Catholic institution. My theme concerns the relative authority attributed to Christ and to culture at institutions of Catholic learning. "All authority in heaven and on earth," the Great Commission says, "has been given to me (Jesus)." How are we to understand this statement in a society as complex as our own? I propose to reflect on the authority of Christ in a culture where authority is constantly and fundamentally contested—and yet always present in various forms.

ASPECTS OF AUTHORITY

In an essay in the *New York Times Book Review*, Robert Jay Lifton and Charles B. Strozier, from the Center on Violence and Human Survival at John Jay College of CUNY, reflected on the 50 million Americans who share a fundamentalist Christian belief that we live in the last days. These fellow citizens consider themselves "reborn" and find inerrant truth in the bible. Their view of the world is represented in Frank Peretti's novel, *This Present Darkness*, which has sold more than a million copies since 1986, and in Charles Colson's several versions of his conversion experience. Both authors offer a dark reading of our present culture. A similar view is represented by James C. Dobson's *Dare to Discipline*, a Christian psychology of the child/parent relation that has sold over 2 million copies since its publication in 1970; and by Billy Graham's ideologically ambitious work, *Facing Death: And The Life After*. But the best-selling representative of these ideas is Hal Lindsey, whose *The Late Great Planet Earth* has sold more than 10 million copies in the United States since it was published in 1970.

Lifton and Strozier show true sympathy for the plight of individual fundamentalists, whose commitment to an imminent end time comes into fairly frequent contradiction with other convictions derived from more reflective experience. But the authors are clearly most concerned about the social influence of this movement, the interaction between a reading of the gospel and its effect on culture. They are wary of a strong tendency in the movement, with it biblically literalist impulse, "to remake the world in its own theocratic image." "Fundamentalism," they note, represents a current in American life that has always lived side by side with, but in considerable opposition to, the Jeffersonian spirit of openness and questioning of authority. It imposes on all matters a quality of ideological totalism—of insistence on all-or-none judgments and positions. Fundamentalism thus exerts an expanding influence in the direction of absoluteness and closure at a time when flexibility and openness to new ideas are desperately required.[9]

In fact, a literal interpretation of the bible and of the authority of Christ has been common since earliest Christianity. In what the great American theologian H. Richard Niebuhr called "radical or exclusive Christianity," an anticultural opposition was set up between Christ and culture. This way of understanding the relationship between the two authorities was exemplified in the ancient world by Tertullian, for example, or in the nineteenth century by Tolstoy.

Niebuhr analyzed this first typical response in his classic work, *Christ and Culture*. A neoorthodox theologian deeply rooted in Christian tradition, Niebuhr was also an inheritor of the great American experiment in religious freedom and pluralism. Before undertaking his scheme of Christian ethical types, he reasonably enough offered a descriptive definition of culture. "Culture," he wrote, is "the 'artificial, secondary environment' which human beings superimpose on the natural."[10] It may be characterized as always social; a human achievement; designed for an end or ends constituting a world of values; concerned especially with the good for human beings. Culture is also always concerned with the temporal and material realization of values and, almost as much, with the conservation of values. Culture, as Niebuhr understood it, is always pluralistic.

Anticultural, radical, or exclusive Christianity was the first "typical" way of relating Christ and culture. Niebuhr also spoke of it as the "Christ against culture" approach. A second evaluation discerned an easier agreement between Christ and culture, a more or less facile accommodation of the two authorities. For such an accommodating Christianity, Christ belongs to culture and is to be found within it—as the Gnostics thought, or Abelard in the Middle Ages, or Albert Ritschl at the end of the nineteenth century. The church, from this perspective, confesses and follows the "Christ *of* culture."

Three other models of the relationship have actually been more prevalent. Niebuhr characterized them as deriving from the church of the center, in which Christ and culture are both distinguished and affirmed. For a "synthetic Christianity," an integration is expected between the surrounding culture and Christ as its exemplary product or result. This view sees "Christ above culture," and typically prizes the achievements of a Clement of Alexandria or a Thomas Aquinas. (Niebuhr himself saw Thomas this way, I believe, in good measure as a result of Leo XIII's naming Thomas as the official theologian of the Catholic church.)

Still a fourth way to relate the authority of the gospel and the authority of culture may be called a "dualist" or "paradoxical" Christianity, as exemplified in St. Paul or Martin Luther. When Christ and culture are understood paradoxically, emphasis is placed on the polarity and tension between them, so that no one set of statements can ever resolve the question of their respective authorities.

A fifth and final type analyzed by Niebuhr represents the situation of what he called "conversionist" or "transformational" Christianity. Here Christ is the one who converts and transforms, calling a culture to its truer self and leading it toward a radically new form. The great models for this view are St. John, Augustine, or F.D. Maurice, all favorite theologians of Niebuhr.

In Niebuhr's interpretation, no one of these types is final and correct. Rather, they represent *typical* answers from the Christian tradition. And while his own preference for a transformational Christianity is fairly apparent, that should not overshadow his genuine appreciation for other modes of dialogue between Christ and culture.

It may be useful for our contemporary situation to ask who some more current representatives of Niebuhr's ethical types might be. What theologians or prominent church members represent these attitudes today? Examples of the first, radical type have been found, I believe, in the Catholic resistance of Daniel Berrigan or James Douglas and also in various forms of the Jesus movement. The Christ of culture has been represented to some extent in the secular Christianity of Leslie Dewart or the earlier Gregory Baum.[11] But then again we find this model also in the White House prayer services, in the culture of the American Legion, or in certain activities of the Knights of Columbus.

I see a synthetic form of Christianity exemplified in Bernard Lonergan or the pastoral pontificate of John Paul II. For current examples of Niebuhr's paradoxical Christianity, a Calvinist theologian such as Jürgen Moltmann or certain liberation theologians such as Rosemary Ruether come to mind. For the conversionist or transformation model, where Christ is seen as a figure calling a culture beyond itself through conversion to its truer achievements and possibilities, one might point to Wolfhart Pannenberg, Karl Rahner, or certain other liberation theologians such as Gustavo Gutierrez or Jon Sobrino.

AUTHORITY AND AMERICAN CULTURE

More recently, other authors have analyzed the relative authority of gospel and culture with particular concern for American society. Avery Dulles, for example, has noted four major stages in the development of American culture—or at least in the white, Anglo-Saxon, Protestant culture that until very recently dominated our national consciousness.[12]

The first movement, the Puritanism of Congregationalist New England, was characterized by a rigorous doctrinal and moral system, biblically grounded, and interpreted in a typically Calvinist mode. If the church had overshadowed all else in Calvin's Geneva, it did so in Boston as well. And even though this Calvinist heritage has now lost most of its power, its memory lives on—so much so that Sidney E. Mead could still speak of the United States in 1975 as the "nation with the soul of a church."[13]

The second state of our cultural development, Dulles suggests, coincides with the nation's founders and the authors of the Declaration of Independence, the Constitution, and the Bill of Rights. By this time in our history, the world view of the Puritans had yielded to that of Christians deeply imbued with the principles of a deistic religion of "nature and of nature's God." In the Declaration of Independence and similar documents, we see how Christian themes and the religion of reason were interwoven. God is understood as the creator and ruler of the universe. God's creatures are endowed with certain inalienable rights that should be accorded universal respect. The young republic's claim to freedom and independence was thus given a transcendent grounding for its commitment to inherited moral and religious standards.

With the rise of individualistic and utilitarian philosophical views in the nineteenth century, a new set of values emerged. Numerous recent studies and conferences have been devoted to liberalism's reconception of the common good as the balancing of competing interests.[14] In Dulles's words, "The Puritan moralism of the 17th century, and the cult of civic virtue in the 18th century, now yielded to a system in which material wealth became the dominant value."[15] Robert Bellah and his coauthors are among the most prominent authors to have emphasized the enduring influence of this movement in our own time.[16]

With the emergence of the United States as the dominant world power in the twentieth century and the advent of the "American century," American culture has undergone further significant transformations. A new mass culture characterized by rapid technological developments, mass communications, and a service economy is reshaping the way Americans imagine themselves. Remnants of a public philosophy persist and minority groups continue to struggle for full participation in the American dream. But an undeniable and pervasive current of consumerism has infected most realms of American life. Indeed, in these last years of the century, many decry the dissolution of the American dream. Our culture's superficiality and lack of historical sense become more painful than ever. In our national leaders, but just as much in ourselves, we notice more often than we would wish a lack of "the courage to be"—that freely venturing, resolute spirit of which Paul Tillich wrote so eloquently at mid-century.[17]

At this juncture, precisely, religious communities and their traditions represent one of the nation's great untapped resources. With regard to Catholicism in particular, Dulles analyzes four major strategies of response. He speaks of them as traditionalist, neoconservative, liberal, and prophetic-radical. The types cross over to a certain extent with Niebuhr's, of course; my point in highlighting them is to indicate how such typologies may be helpful in understanding the role of various, competing authorities in contemporary life.

STRATEGIES OF RESPONSE

For a traditionalist mentality, Dulles notes, the prevailing cultural trends are in need of serious criticism. Nostalgic for a more centralized and authoritarian Catholicism, traditionalists insist on enduring values and transcendent symbolism. One may find moderate examples of this approach in James Hitchcock or Ralph Martin, and a more extreme example in a figure such as Archbishop Lefebvre.

A neoconservative movement is well represented by authors such as George Weigel or Michael Novak, for whom natural reason and civil argument are primary values. Such authors see it as the first task of the church to proclaim and live the gospel, but they regard it as their own task to seek above all the renewal of American democracy. They understand the church as providentially granted a great opportunity vis-à-vis culture, namely, to construct "a religiously informed public philosophy for the American experiment in ordered liberty."[18]

By using its resources wisely and courageously, this strategy hopes to fulfill what theologian Richard John Neuhaus, then still a Lutheran, in 1987 hailed as the "Catholic moment." (Pastor Neuhaus has since converted to Catholicism.) In sometimes polemical dialogue with authors who are more critical of capitalism, the neoconservatives argue that democratic capitalism can significantly enrich Catholic teaching on political economy. When in fact it does not, they view Catholic social teaching as having erred more or less seriously.

A third strategy, Catholic liberalism, looks to the American experience to help bring the church into the modern age. Participation and subsidiarity, dialogue and democratization are key concepts for authors such as Jay Dolan and Dennis McCann. If neoconservatives are primarily interested in reforming society and expect the church to exercise its authority on the surrounding culture, liberals are as likely to turn to the culture for resources with which to reform the church. A natural and appropriate authority is thus attributed to culture in dialogue with the gospel. (Indeed, and with good reason, many commentators have emphasized that the recent pastoral letters written by the United States bishops on peace and the economy have been just as important for their dialogic method as for the direct content of their teaching. By regularly consulting the community of the church on the topics under discussion, they have encouraged and empowered a more open form of moral argument.)

A fourth contemporary version of the relation between gospel and culture can be called radical Catholicism. Years ago, Dorothy Day turned from communism to the church as a place where she could work more effectively for peace and the poor. Since the 1960s, Daniel Berrigan, S.J., has participated in numerous countercultural protests, often appealing to the Book of Revelation as a text that teaches us to set the cross against the world. More recently still, Matthew Fox has advocated a creation-centered spirituality that sees itself in opposition to the evils he vehemently decries in contemporary society—capitalism, militarism, racism, sexism, the abuse of native peoples. Such radical Catholics are seldom comfortable with any establishment, whether secular or ecclesiastical. Often they are also stunningly aware of the power of the biblical word, which many of the rest of us too easily assume we have heard.

CONTRAST OF STRATEGIES

The strategies can be compared rather neatly. Neoconservatives strongly affirm both Catholicism and American secular culture. Radicals point to the corruption in both. Catholic traditionalists view ecclesiastical culture as holy but the secular culture as debased. Liberals consider the American experiment to be providential, and traditional Catholicism sees it in need of providential reform.

Traditionalists typically have a strong ecclesial sense and are naturally attracted to "thinking with the church." On the other hand, they are tempted to be nostalgic in an unhistorical way and frequently fail to recognize the difficulty of contemporary questions. While they rightly remind us of the church's ancient wisdom, they risk finding its future in other worldliness.

To the traditionalists' strong sense of the church, neoconservatives add a vivid sense of American values. They easily overlook the individualistic isolation of American life, however, and the decline of a commitment to the common good in American society. In addition, their recommendations are often thin with respect to ways of renewing faith in the coming of the kingdom of God.

Liberals, again, have high esteem for the particularities of the American experience. They are also deeply aware of the secular context in which the church always exists; it is always in a particular world situation that the church proclaims the gospel amid the struggle between good and evil. But liberals, at their best, also recognize that the church too is always a church of sinners. On the other hand, liberals typically risk politicization of religious values, partisanship in politics, and, ecclesiastically, an excess of anti-Roman affect. They can be ahistorical in their own way, seeming to forget that Catholics belong to a church of the ages as well as of the world. It is never easy to balance secular consciousness with rigorous attention to the inner life of faith and a vibrant spirituality.

Radicals, finally, rightly cultivate a sense for the prophetic, an enduring appreciation of the church's need for repentance and reform. In their emphasis on apocalyptic views of the world, however, they regularly neglect the incarnational character of Catholicism. In that case, eschatology or the doctrine of God's final judgment on world history becomes instead a denunciation or ideology of the insufficiency of all secular values.

For Dulles, the pivotal issue in these discussions about the authority of Christ and the authority of culture on the contemporary scene is "whether the church in this country should become more countercultural, as the traditionalists and radicals would wish, or more accommodationist, as the liberals and some neo-conservatives propose." Should the church, in other words, oppose our culture or work with it for commonly perceived goals? While recognizing the great benefit of American traditions with regard to freedom, personal initiative, open communication, and active participation, Dulles nevertheless argues that "Catholics will be well advised to cultivate a measured, prudent counterculturalism."[19] When pressed for a declaration of loyalty, he instinctively considers that it must be to the church and the gospel.

TYPES AND SIGNS

Dulles has refined his view in subsequent publications, but his original essay already clearly raised the question of Christ and culture in a significantly helpful way for our contemporary American context, and in particular for many discussions currently under way in Catholic higher education. Like Niebuhr before him, he serves as a paradigmatic theologian and also, if to a lesser extent, as an insightful interpreter of culture. With Niebuhr as well, his typological thinking intends not merely to lay out different positions, to compare and contrast them, but rather to mediate between them. Rather than choosing one position over another, he helps the proponents of each to see the strengths of the other, so that the partners in the dialogue may incorporate each other's viewpoints into their own way of thinking and move beyond the stale impasse of opposing positions.

Each of these authors recognizes the complexity of discipleship and citizenship in our pluralist society. All see how difficult it is both to follow Christ as Lord and to participate as mature citizens in our nation's life. Indeed, the permanence of this challenge in the modern era has been signalized by the socially most farsighted document of the Second Vatican Council, "The Pastoral Constitution of the Church in the Modern World." It is also underlined by Paul VI's great apostolic letter, *Evangelii Nuntiandi*, on the proclamation of the gospel.

But how can we draw today on the strengths and weaknesses, the advantages and disadvantages of the various models? What might break through the multiple possibilities they offer and lead us to wise decision? The models cannot be, after all, simply a way of understanding the different relationships between Christ and culture. Niebuhr especially emphasized that he was analyzing ethical types. What might lead us then to wise decisions about the various relationships? Our position on this matter will be important for understanding both society and the church, humanity and its God.

Let me suggest that one way to use the types well, adding a perspective that is perhaps less prominent in Dulles's analysis, would be to give greater importance to the "signs of the times" and the reform of our lives as we seek to read them. In our efforts to interpret both the gospel and our culture, we hope to respond to the values of the gospel and the needs of our culture. But we are likewise called to respond to the values of the culture and the needs to which the gospel alerts us. Values and answers cannot simply be located on one side of the dialogue, while needs and questions are relegated to the other. As we recognize the complex interaction of both, we must combine understanding and choice, reflective intelligence and just action. In other words, the theoretical constructs of the various types of relationship between gospel and culture need to be complemented by the imperatives of practice; the relation we find obtaining between gospel and culture must be enacted in some form of transformative action. To put it another way, *typical* answers to the dialogue of gospel and culture become less pure when they are tested in practice.

As Monika Hellwig has pointed out, the questions of any time strongly influence how the very foundations of theology are once again built.[20] As I have suggested earlier, our own American Catholic bishops have offered us practical ways to respond to urgent contemporary questions. In several major pastoral letters, they have analyzed leading issues of our day, inspired by the gospel but firmly situated in the culture. In 1983 they published "The Challenge of Peace" on the question of nuclear arms and peace. In 1986 they presented "Economic Justice for All," arguing that the discrepancy of the economic situation in the United States was insupportable. In November 1989, they published the "Pastoral Plan for Black Catholics." (Unfortunately, after having considered a document on concerns of women in church and society for almost a decade, they have not been able to agree on a statement.) In each of these efforts, they have analyzed the signs of the times and asked Catholics to become more aware of the evils of nuclearism, economic injustice, racism, and sexism. Having read their letters, one hears the voice of Christ in the scriptures ringing with a new urgency.[21]

One might argue perhaps that the content of these letters is elicited by social need, while their dialogic method is suggested by God's word addressing that need. On the contrary, I would argue that content and method in the pastoral letters are inseparably linked, as regards both gospel and culture. It is certainly not the gospel alone that inculcates a dialogic understanding of human existence. The relationship between Jesus and his disciples, and still more the prayer of Jesus to his God, suggest dialogue as the essence of life. But American experience also clearly places great emphasis on open and free communication. Likewise, while the bishops have been led by evangelical motives to denounce nuclearism, economic inequity, racism, and sexism, they have also been strongly influenced by the society around them in looking for ways in which those social ills might be remedied.

It is unlikely, then, that we can finally adopt a single method for relating Christ and culture as the authorities in our lives. Rather, we may be helped by various analyses of the different ways they relate. We break through the problem of choosing one typical response or another according as we focus on a pressing issue of our time. The key will be to listen both to the gospel as God's word addressing our time and to our time as God's creation meant to be transformed by God's word.

Our bishops, for example, will certainly have authoritative words, but seldom *final* words, to say to us on these social questions. Our culture will develop the very context of the language in which the religious message can be heard. Will we remain open to God's word and subject to it? Will our bishops, as the "Dogmatic Constitution on Divine Revelation" emphasizes, be able to help us to remain subject to the word of God and not above it?[22] Will our culture, on the other hand, awaken us to the devaluation of words as well as individuals, the plethora of symbols and the need to be critical of our pluralistic tradition? Matters such as these are never static but always dynamic, just as our understanding of the relation between God's word and our life is never static but always dynamic. Even the Word of God incarnate is not fixed once and for all, but grows through time, above all as his sufferings are completed in our own.

CONCLUSION

In closing, let me risk offering some guidelines to assist our careful attention to the dialogue we have been discussing. Recognizing with both Professor Niebuhr and Father Dulles that the great Christian tradition is always larger than our interpretations of it, and recognizing also that the signs of the times often require more urgent response than may be comfortable, I think it can be reasonably assumed that

1. No one "typical" response to the dialogue between gospel and culture is ever adequate. Whenever we absolutize one way of understanding the relationship, we overlook genuine strengths of other possibilities. Accordingly, we should allow the dialogue to be as comprehensive as possible, well aware of its complexity.
2. We should beware of understanding the gospel and the church primarily as "countercultural." The prophetic element is central to Christianity, and all culture is in need of reform. But much in American life inherently favors religion, and much is humanly positive.
3. We should also beware of "cultural enthusiasm." Although freedom of religion and a natural piety have accompanied our republic from its foundation, the gospel transcends any one culture, and the kingdom of God can never be identified with any one phase of history.
4. We should avoid reducing the dialogue between gospel and culture to a single issue. There are gospel values that can never be compromised, just as there are cultural attainments that deserve strong loyalty. But the most wholehearted discipleship and the most responsible citizenship nevertheless remain the witness of imperfect men and women whose failures on one score should not denigrate their whole lives. Integralism is ultimately a formula not for fidelity but for rigidity.
5. We should learn from the church's historical breadth. In its service to the word of God through the centuries, the church has incalculable lessons of patience, tolerance, and endurance to teach. Her forbearance with her members is entirely different from laxist morality or doctrinal indifferentism. She knows the power of anathemas and excommunications, but has far more

often succeeded with the *discreta caritas* of cogent rhetoric and prudent discipline.

6. Politics and prayer, mysticism and worldliness are inseparable moments in the dialogue. While it may be thought that prayer and a mystical sense pertain to the gospel and that a worldly sense of the human community derives from the culture, it is just as true that God's word shows us the world in its true light and that the city of humanity at its heart longs to become the city of God.

7. We should leave all *final* judgment to God, our creator and redeemer. Even our bishops must do this. We are challenged to read the signs of our times and respond to them as truly believing Christians. That shapes the crucible in which we concretize the authorities of Christ and culture in our lives. But the ultimate verdict on the success of our efforts occurs only when all authority becomes Christ's and Christ becomes God's in that consummation of history we hope to see in the realized kingdom of God. Until that time, we must all make the most responsible decisions of which we are capable. Our bishops remain our official pastors and teachers. But the Holy Spirit is given to all Christians to guide their lives, and final judgment belongs to the Lord.

For many of us Christ is, in a very real sense, the absolute authority in our lives. But for all of us as well, American culture is an authority of inestimable value. Perhaps as we encourage a conversation between the two, with an eye to the most pressing issues of our age, we may find new ways proudly to be American citizens and humbly to continue becoming disciples of Christ.

                    *   *   *

Note: The above essay is a revised version of a paper originally presented in the Warren Lecture Series at the University of Tulsa on September 16, 1990, and printed here with permission.

NOTES

1. Karl Rahner, "Basic Theological Interpretation of the Second Vatican Council," in *Concern for the Church: Theological Investigations 22*, trans. Edward Quinn (New York: Crossroad, 1981), 77-89.

2. Cf. George Gallup, Jr., and Jim Castelli, *The American Catholic People: Their Beliefs, Practices and Values* (Garden City, New York: Doubleday, 1987); Leo J. O'Donovan, S.J., "Many Worlds and One World: Georgetown and the

Society of Jesus in Their American Context," in William J. O'Brien, ed., *Splendor and Wonder: Jesuit Character, Georgetown Spirit, and Liberal Education* (Washington, D.C.: Georgetown University Press, 1988), 85-106; Leo J. O'Donovan, S.J., "Die Krise ernst nehmen—Die Vereinigten Staaten als Kontext öffentlicher Theologie," in Karl Heinz Neufeld, ed., *Probleme und Perspektiven Dogmatischer Theologie* (Düsseldorf: Patmos, 1986), 440-459.

3. "Celebrating Two Centuries of Education," *America*, 20 May 1989: 467.

4. Cf. John P. Langan, S.J., ed., *Catholic Universities in Church and Society: A Dialogue on "Ex Corde Ecclesiae"* (Washington, D.C.: Georgetown University Press, 1993).

5. Text in *Origins* vol. 18, no. 40 (16 March 1989): 661, 663. Cf. Report of the Catholic Theological Society of America Committee on the Profession of Faith and the Oath of Fidelity (Catholic Theological Society of America, 1990).

6. Text in *Origins*, vol. 20, no. 8 (5 July 1990): 117, 119-126.

7. Cf. Richard A. McCormick, S.J., *The Critical Calling: Reflections on Moral Dilemmas Since Vatican II* (Washington, D.C.: Georgetown University Press, 1989).

8. Edward A. Malloy, "Church Finances in Crisis: How Catholic Higher Education Can Help," *America*, vol. 163, no. 5 (1 September 1990): 104-105.

9. *New York Times Book Review*, 12 August 1990, 25; previous quote at p. 24. Cf. Thomas F. O'Meara, O.P., *Fundamentalism: A Catholic Perspective* (Mahwah, New Jersey: Paulist, 1990).

10. H. Richard Niebuhr *Christ and Culture* (New York: Harper, 1951), 32. For further discussion of the notion of culture, cf. Clifford Geertz, *The Interpretation of Cultures* (New York: Basic Books, 1973); Ian Robertson, *Sociology* (New York: Worth, 1987), chap. 5, "Culture"; William J. Byron, S.J., "Between Church and Culture: A Role for Catholic Higher Education," *Thought*, vol. 66, no. 262 (September 1991): 310-316.

11. Cf. Mary Jo Leddy, N.D.S., and Mary Ann Hinsdale, I.H.M., eds., *Faith That Transforms: Essays in Honor of Gregory Baum* (Mahwah, New Jersey: Paulist, 1987).

12. For the following pages, see Dulles's article "Catholicism and American Culture: The Uneasy Dialogue," *America*, vol. 162, no. 3 (27 January 1990): 54-59.

13. Sidney E. Mead, *The Nation with the Soul of a Church* (New York: Harper and Row, 1975).

14. Cf. R. Bruce Douglass, Gerald M. Mara, and Henry S. Richardson, eds., *Liberalism and the Good* (New York: Routledge, 1990).

15. Dulles, "Catholicism and American Culture," 55.

16. Cf. Robert Bellah et al., *Habits of the Heart: Individualism and Commitment in American Life* (Berkeley: University of California Press, 1985) and *The Good Society* (New York: Knopf, 1991).

17. *The Courage to Be* (New Haven: Yale University Press, 1952). Cf. Leo J. O'Donovan, S.J., "The Pasch of Christ: Our Courage in Time," *Theological Studies* 42 (1981): 353-372.

18. Dulles, "Catholicism and American Culture," 56.

19. Ibid., 59. See also Dulles's "Cattolicesimo e Cultura Americana: Un Dialogo Difficile," *La Civiltà cattolica*, 7 July 1990 (Quindicinale Anno 141 3361): 16-25.

20. "Foundations for Theology: A Historical Sketch," in Leo J. O'Donovan and T. Howland Sanks, eds., *Faithful Witness: Foundations of Theology for Today's Church* (New York: Crossroad, 1989), 1-13.

21. Cf. Philip J. Murnion, ed., *Catholics and Nuclear War: A Commentary on "The Challenge of Peace"* (New York: Crossroad, 1983); Judith A. Dwyer, ed., *The Catholic Bishops and Nuclear War: A Critique and Analysis of the Pastoral "The Challenge of Peace"* (Washington, D.C.: Georgetown University Press, 1984); R. Bruce Douglass, ed., *The Deeper Meaning of Economic Life: Critical Essays on the U.S. Catholic Bishops' Pastoral Letter on the Economy* (Washington, D.C.: Georgetown University Press, 1986).

22. *Dei Verbum*, art. 10.

2

"Tradition in Transition"

My title is redundant. For surely Jaroslav Pelikan is correct when he notes that one of the marks of a living tradition is "its capacity to develop while still maintaining its identity and continuity."[1] In a real sense, then, tradition is always in transition. To think otherwise is to confuse tradition (the living faith of the dead) with traditionalism (the dead faith of the living).

To be instructed by the past without being enslaved by it requires the capacity to dream. In a sense, everyone has a dream these days. Cardinal Basil Hume reported one at the Synod of 1980.[2] Martin Luther King had one. Karl Rahner wrote about his in 1981.[3] The dream format is a remarkably useful vehicle. For one thing, it brings the imagination into theology, and that is not all bad. For another, it allows one to float what may appear to be unthinkable, unconventional, and astonishing ideas without completely owning them. One can, as it were, be preposterous without being possessive. After all, "it was only a dream."

Yet today's reveries sometimes turn out to be tomorrow's realities. Thank God! Without dreamers where would we be? In this sense, it can be argued that our responsibility, an aspect of our share in providence,[4] is to dream—that is, to foresee options and possibilities in order to burst the bonds of conventionality and allow Christianity not only to remember the past but to create the future and thereby to meet the theological and pastoral needs of the believing community. It was in this spirit that Archbishop Rembert Weakland stated that "we are living at a time when we must re-imagine the Catholic church. We must examine our own moral convictions, work through them in the light of the Gospel so that we hold them deeply for ourselves."[5]

I confess that I like the phrase "reimagine the Catholic church." It has a bouncy and daring optimism to it that ought to signalize believers in the Lord. It is a tacit acknowledgement that we can be and often are corporately slovenly. Specifically, we tend to face new problems and challenges by leaning on ancient pillars. We are *laudatores temporis acti*. Andrew Greeley had something like this notion in mind when he reported the defection of one out of ten Hispanic Catholics to Protestant denominations. Greeley likened the response of Catholic officialdom to this startling phenomenon to that of an average, overweight, slightly punch-drunk linebacker. "Despite its size and its strength it lacks the quickness and creativity to respond to challenges."[6]

"Reimagining the Catholic church" sounds radical and revolutionary. Therefore, it is important to understand what it does and does not mean. Reimagining does not refer to an aimless, destructive, change-for-the-sake-of-change dismantling. That is a road to nowhere. Reimagining suggests a more creative and imaginative use of substantials already in place. In this sense it is radical—a recovery of roots (*radix*) long hidden by the barnacled accumulations of custom, habit, and cultural overlay.

Now if we must reimagine the Catholic church to keep it vital and vigorous in changing times, something similar must surely be said about moral theology within the Catholic church. Moral theology is concerned with the behavioral implications of our "being in the Lord." If that very "being" can be twisted and deformed by human caprice, pride, blindness, passion, anthropomorphism, and a host of other distortions, so can its behavioral implications, as John Mahoney, S.J., has recently pointed out in rich detail.[7]

In what follows, then, I want to outline and develop ten characteristics of moral theology as I would hope to find it in the year 2000. Such a reimagining involves all sorts of human exercises: hoping, critiquing the past and present, regretting, aspiring, dreaming. None of this is immune from caricature. If caricature occurs, all I can do is reemphasize that that is the way it is with dreams.

1. CHRISTOCENTRISM AND CHARITY

I dare say that the vast majority of Catholics, when they think of morality and the moral life, think of moral problems, of the rightness and wrongness of certain actions or omissions. Thus: Is premarital sex always wrong? Is it wrong to withhold or withdraw artificial nutrition and hydration from a patient in a persistent vegetative state? Is it wrong to threaten nuclear retaliation? Is it always wrong to speak falsehoods? And on and on. In this spirit, a writer in the *New York Times* recently offered "four simple principles that can help analyze and resolve the ethical dilemmas that often characterize business competition."[8] These were presented as "practical guides" to "being ethical."

"Being ethical," in other words, was conceived as a predicate of "business activities." In short, we identify ethics with dilemma or quandary ethics.

The reasons for such an identification are fairly clear. Cases are newsworthy eye-catchers. They get the headlines and arouse curiosity, and they are amenable to legal wrangling and resolution. Furthermore, they provide a congenial meeting place for people who otherwise have little in common and little to share. Everybody has an opinion on abortion, on drugs, on first use of nuclear weapons, on apartheid, on *in vitro* fertilization. And why not? We are moral beings, and this is the stuff of morality.

Well, not quite. An ethics that claims to be theological will root itself in God—God's actions and purposes. Its primary referents will be God's relation to us, and ours to God. The prime analogate—to use scholastic language—of the term "morality" will be this relationship. The most basic, though not the only, language of theological ethics builds around goodness and badness, not rightness and wrongness of actions, since goodness-badness is basically vertical and has its aortal lifeline to the God-relationship.

In slightly different words, a Christian theological ethic is founded on the fact that something *has been done* to and for us, and that something is Jesus. There is a prior action of God at once revelatory and response-engendering. This prior action of God is reflected in the Pauline "therefore," which states the entire grounding and meaning of the Christian ethic. The Italian theologian Enrico Chiavacci puts it this way:

> In the New Testament, the unique obligation of charity, which is the giving of self to God who is seen in one's neighbor, is grounded on the unique fact that God is charity. . . . "Walk in love as Christ has loved us and given himself" (Eph. 5:2). "Therefore, I exhort you, brethren, through the mercy of God to offer yourselves . . ." (Rom 12:1). The fact that God—in his manifestation as philanthropy—is love does not refer to further justification; it is the ultimate fact. The obligation to love is based only on God's love for us. . . . It is true . . . that in the "therefore" of Romans 12:1 we find the entire New Testament ethic.[9]

When I mention Christian theological ethics, I think primarily of this kind of foundation.

I stress this point because there has been, and still is, a tendency to conceive of Christian ethics primarily in terms of norms and principles that may be derived from Jesus' pronouncements. There are such

sayings recorded in the New Testament. But to reduce Christian ethics
to such sayings is to trivialize it. When the Christian thinks of Christian
ethics (or moral theology—I treat them as identical here), he or she
thinks primarily of what Jesus has done to and for us, and therefore of
who we are. In Joseph Sittler's words:

> He (Jesus) did not, after the manner proper to philosophers of the
> good, attempt to articulate general principles which, once stated,
> have then only to be beaten out in corollaries applicable to the
> variety of human life. . . . His words and deeds belong together.
> Both are signs which seek to fasten our attention upon the single
> vitality which was the ground and purpose of his life—his God-
> relationship."[10]

In and through Jesus we know what that God-relationship is: total self-
gift. For that is what God is and we are created in God's image. To miss
this point is, I believe, to leave the realm of Christian ethics.

To see Jesus at the heart of moral theology is to say that charity is
its heart and soul. For Jesus is the charity of the Father enfleshed. That
is why I have always found Sittler's phrase—"the shape of the engen-
dering deed"—so apt as a description of the structure of Christian ethics.

Yet it is so easy to forget this insight. There are four factors at
work that can easily obscure this centrality of charity: casuistry,
appeals to the natural law, emphasis on the magisterium, and the
importance of philosophical ethics. Each of these factors plays an
indispensable role in the full elaboration of Christian morality. Christian love must become "inprincipled," as the late Paul Ramsey used to
say, and then be applied in a consistent and disciplined way to a host
of intransigent and complex situations. Otherwise it remains at the
level of pious fireside generalization. Similarly, the natural moral law
is not a competitor with charity for jurisdictional primacy in Christian
ethics. Natural law—we can deplore the word—has reference to those
intelligible constants of the human person that delineate the minimal
demands of charitable action.

As for the magisterium, Catholics treasure it as a privileged
source of moral enlightenment. Something similar can be said of moral
philosophy. It brings to moral reflection the analytic clarities and preci-
sion of reasoned discourse.

Yet, unless I am mistaken, the importance of these factors can be
and has been overstated in such a way that each distorts Christian
morality into unrecognizability. Casuistry can easily become legalistic
minimalism. Respect for the magisterium easily converts into a funda-

mentalistic magisteriolotry that breeds conformism. Philosophy too often turns up as a poorly disguised and sterile rationalism. And the natural law is contaminated by the many caricatures noted by John Courtney Murray.[11]

When these distortions occur, the simplicity and splendor of a moral theology—and pastoral catechesis—anchored in and dominated by charity gets hopelessly blurred. Enamored of the parts, we grow blind to the whole. That is why it is still timely—indeed urgent—to dream of a moral theology in the year 2000 that can recover and reproduce the glorious and demanding simplicity of its founder.

2. UNIVERSALITY

As I dream of moral theology in the year 2000, I dream of a presentation of the moral life that will be appealing and make sense to Christians of many cultures. The church is, as Rahner noted, a world church.[12] I will refer to this characteristic of Christian morality as its "universalizing feature." I mean to underline the idea that Christian morality, while being theological to its core, must not be isolationist or sectarian. Isolating accounts of the Christian story would repudiate a constant of the Catholic tradition: God's self-revelation in Jesus does not obliterate the human but illuminates it. As Vatican II worded it: "Faith throws a new light on everything, manifests God's design for man's total vocation, and thus directs the mind to solutions which are *fully human.*"[13] It added: "Whoever follows after Christ, the perfect man, *becomes himself more of a man.*"[14] Christian ethics, then, is the objectification in Jesus Christ of what every person experiences as a subject. In a sense we may say that the resources of scripture, dogma, and Christian life are the fullest available "objectifications" of the common human experience. Neglecting this runs afoul, at some point, of the Chalcedonian formulae about the true humanity of Jesus.

Catholic tradition has attempted, very clumsily at times, to capture this dimension of morality by reference to a natural moral law. I mention this dimension of Christian morality because it has come under attack by several influential writers. For instance, Stanley Hauerwas asserts that the renovation of moral theology called for by Vatican II has not occurred because of a lack of appreciation for the narrative character of Christian moral reflection.[15] Rather, the new "liberal" moral theologians continue to use the basic natural-law methodology of neo-Scholasticism but with the language of human experience. This methodology of "universalistic laws," desires, and tendencies fails to take as fundamental the community and thus its narrative context. This failure leads to a failure in pastoral practice.

Hauerwas then points out the direction of a true Christian ethic. Narratives are essential for our understanding of God, ourselves, and the world. The central claim of Christian ethics is that we know ourselves truthfully only when we know ourselves in relation to God. Our participation in God's life is a participation in the history God creates, God's story. And that story is particularistic, that is, it deals with Israel, Jesus, and the ingathering of disciples we name the church. "Christian ethics is, therefore, not an ethic based on universal presuppositions that can be known separate from these particular peoples' traditions." Rather, it is "the discipline that attempts to remind us of the kind of skills, linguistic, conceptual and practical, that are necessary to be such a people." (I pause parenthetically to wonder how Christianity, in Hauerwas's reading, could ever have been preached to the Gentiles.)

How does this perspective affect practical problem-solving? Hauerwas insists that its effect should be to direct our attention away from "dilemma ethics." The first question in pastoral care is not "What should I do?" but "What should I be?" Furthermore, this perspective helps to make the church's stance about marriage and divorce more intelligible. This stand as absolute is not intelligible. It must be seen as an aid to help us live more nearly faithful to the story that forms the Christian community. It functions as a reminder of what kind of "virtues are necessary to sustain a Christian people to carry on the story of God." Christian ethics, understood in this narrative way, is deeply antithetical to the natural-law method of Catholic moral theology. It does not pretend to be based on a universally valid stand applicable to all persons irrespective of their story. In this sense it may be called sectarian.

I agree with many of Hauerwas's emphases. But there is one that I cannot accept: Hauerwas's contrast between an ethic built on a particular narrative and one of "universalistic laws." This emphasis is also explicit in John Howard Yoder's work. Such a position cuts reality too sharply. To assert that certain basic obligations or duties apply across the board to persons as persons is not an indication, as Hauerwas maintains, that one has failed to take community and its narrative context as fundamental. Nor is it, as Yoder asserts, "motivated . . . by embarrassment about particularity."[16] It is to argue something about the human condition that we think is generally knowable if our story is to include, for example, Romans 1.

The root of the dichotomy Hauerwas and Yoder assert between narrative and "universalizing" morality is the particularizing and exclusive character they give the story—as if the incarnate word of God had nothing to do with or to say about those persons who never lived that particular story. Thus I would guess—possibly erroneously—that

Hauerwas's phrase "faithfulness to this man as a guide," which he correctly says is "morally central to Christian ethics," means that others simply cannot share *any* of the insights and judgments such faithfulness generates. Otherwise, why the overstated contrast between narrative and "universalizing" tendencies, and the attack on the latter? I question that. There is no contradiction between being countercultural and yet culturally intelligible. Similarly, when Yoder sees a focus on generalizability as forgetting that "we confess as Lord and Christ the man Jesus,"[17] he is giving this confession a practical ethical content unavailable to those outside the confession.

Whatever the case, this exclusive dichotomizing is not the Catholic reading and living of the story. Roger Shinn makes this point very well. He notes that the ethical awareness given to Christians in Christ "meets some similar intimations or signs of confirmation in wider human experience." Christians believe, Shinn writes, that the *Logos* made flesh in Christ is the identical *Logos* through which the world was created. He concludes: "They [Christians] do not expect the Christian faith and insight to be confirmed by unanimous agreement of all people, even all decent and idealistic people. But they do expect the fundamental Christian motifs to have some persuasiveness in general experience."[18] It is this "same persuasiveness in general experience" that can found confidence in the possibility of public moral discourse, a possibility Hauerwas and Yoder distrust and eventually disdain.

Therefore, when I dream of Christian ethics in the year 2000, I dream of one that is confident of its ability to communicate intelligibly to a broader (than the church) society.

3. SUBSIDIARITY

The term "subsidiarity" was first used, to the best of my knowledge, by Pius XI in *Quadragesimo anno*. He stated:

> Just as it is gravely wrong to take from individuals what they can accomplish by their own initiative and industry and give it to the community, so also it is an injustice and at the same time a grave evil and disturbance of right order to assign to a greater and higher association what lesser and subordinate organizations can do.[19]

Clearly Pius XI was speaking of subsidiarity within the context of the legitimate but limited role of the state.

When I use the term of moral theology, I am obviously using it in an analogous sense. That sense refers above all to development of

moral policy and decision-making. It suggests that higher, more centralized authority should not assume all responsibilities in these areas
and thus relieve local authorities (e.g., national episcopal conferences)
or individuals of their proper responsibilities.

This point can be made in any number of ways. I will use the distinction between principle and application to illumine it.

Some popes (Pius XI, Pius XII, John XXIII) spoke in rather sweep-
ing terms about the church's teaching competence, extending it quite
indiscriminately to the whole moral law, including applications.

A remarkably different approach begins to appear with Vatican
II. The bishops provide guidelines for the interpretation of the *Pastoral
Constitution on the Church in the Modern World*. They state that "in part
two [where special urgent moral problems are treated] the subject matter which is viewed in the light of doctrinal principles is made up of
diverse elements. Some elements have a permanent value; others, only
a transitory one. . . . Interpreters must bear in mind—especially in part
two—the changeable circumstances which the subject matter, by its
very nature, involves."[20]

The Council further noted that "it happens rather frequently, and
legitimately so, that with equal sincerity some of the faithful will disagree with others on a given matter."[21] This legitimate pluralism is to
be expected if even official teachers do not have all the answers, a point
explicitly made by the Council:

> The Church guards the heritage of God's Word and draws from it
> religious and moral principles, without always having at hand
> the solution to particular problems. She desires thereby to add
> the light of revealed truth to mankind's store of experience, so
> that the path which humanity has taken in recent times will not
> be a dark one.[22]

This *nouvelle modestie* did not escape the notice of the American
bishops. In *The Challenge of Peace* they explicitly stress the difference
between universal moral principles and their applications:

> We stress here at the beginning that not every statement in this
> letter has the same moral authority. At times we reassert univer-
> sally binding moral principles (e.g., noncombatant immunity and
> proportionality). At still other times we reaffirm statements of
> recent popes and the teaching of Vatican II. Again, at other times
> we apply moral principles to specific cases.[23]

The bishops note that where applications are concerned "prudential judgments are involved based on specific circumstances which can
change or which can be interpreted differently by people of good will."

They conclude that their judgments of application should be taken seriously but are "not binding in conscience."

Applications of moral principle demand special expertise and knowledge of circumstances; therefore, they should be entrusted above all to those who have such knowledge and expertise. When a higher authority (whether it be the Congregation for the Doctrine of the Faith, a local bishop, a pastor) attempts to assume this role, we have a violation of subsidiarity. One of the results of this violation is that the church is deprived of the richness of experience and thought some of its members can contribute. Another is the promotion of a kind of moral infantilism.

It was in this spirit that Vatican II issued its summons to lay people:

> Laymen should also know that it is generally the function of their well-formed Christian conscience to see that the divine law is inscribed in the life of the earthly city. From priests they may look for spiritual light and nourishment. Let the layman not imagine that his pastors are always such experts, that to every problem which arises, however complicated, they can readily give him a concrete solution, or even that such is their mission. Rather, enlightened by Christian wisdom and giving close attention to the teaching authority of the Church, let the layman take on his own distinctive role.[24]

I confess that this is one of my favorite conciliar texts, not because it lightens the workload of moral theologians, but because it summarizes and symbolizes so many other things—theological things—the Council was striving to do. High on the list of these things was toppling the pyramidal notion of the church wherein truth descends uniquely from above in a kind of mysterious paternalistic flow.

In this citation I believe we can legitimately read two assertions. First, conscience cannot be utterly preprogrammed. Second, laypeople have special competencies, and therefore special responsibilities. Physicians, for example, by virtue of their special expertise, should reflect on and pray over the moral and specifically Christian dimensions of their vocation and bring the fruits of their reflection to the entire church. If they do not, where do we get such insights? This is the burden of the phrase "distinctive role." It is an example of what I mean by subsidiarity in moral theology.

4. PERSONALISM

I use this term in a specific sense and in a quite restrictive context. The context is the determination of the morally right and morally wrong of human actions. The specific sense is that the human person in all facets and dimensions is the criterion of this moral rightfulness and wrongfulness. That formulation is meant to contrast with an approach that employs an isolated dimension of the human person as criterion.

I do not think it is unfair to say that some earlier Catholic approaches fell into this trap. John Courtney Murray referred to this one-sidedness as the "biologist interpretation" and argued that it confused the "primordial," in a biological sense, with the natural.[25] Thus we find Franciscus Hürth, S.J., an influential advisor to Pius XI and Pius XII, laying heavy stress on biological facticity. "The will of nature" he says, "was inscribed in the organs and their functions." He concludes:

> Man only has disposal of the use of his organs and faculties with respect to the end which the Creator, in His formation of them, has intended. This end for man, then, is both the biological law and the moral law, such that the latter obliges him to live according to the biological law.[26]

For this reason, John C. Ford, S.J., and Gerald Kelly, S.J., wrote in 1963: "One cannot exaggerate the importance attached to the physical integrity of the act itself both in papal documents and in Catholic theology generally."[27]

Vatican II moved beyond such "physical integrity" when it proposed as criterion "the person integrally and adequately considered." As Louis Janssens words it: "From a personalist standpoint what must be examined is what the intervention as a whole means for the promotion of the human persons who are involved and for their relationships."[28]

I mention this personalism as a component of my dream because, while it is explicitly honored in some recent official documents (e.g., *Donum vitae*, the document of the Congregation for the Doctrine of Faith (CDF) on reproductive technologies), many of us believe that an older biologism reappears when (indeed, whenever) there is question of specific conclusions and applications.

5. MODESTY AND TENTATIVENESS

In Rahner's dream, the pope is imagined as saying:

> On the one hand the ordinary magisterium of the pope in authentic doctrinal decisions at least in the past and up to very recent times was often involved in error and, on the other hand, Rome

was accustomed to put forward and insist on such decisions as if there could be no doubt about their ultimate correctness and as if any further discussion of them was unbecoming for a Catholic theologian.[29]

This hubris is not just the *stylus curiae*. It seems to be a perennial temptation of those who exercise both jurisdictional and teaching authority. There is the seemingly irresistible penchant to prescribe and proscribe *urbi et orbi* with utter certainty and forever, as though teaching would not be taken seriously unless it is proposed for all ages.

Thus, for example, in the CDF's *Inner insigniores* (1976) the norm of not ordaining women to the priesthood is said to be observed "because it is considered to conform to God's plan for his church."[30] That is a theological lock-in. It is quite possible, I believe, to oppose ordination of women (I hasten to say that I do not) for reasons and with analyses other than that.

We are all aware of the genuine complexity of many human moral problems. My dream, therefore, is that acknowledgement of this complexity will take the form of appropriate modesty and tentativeness in authentic church teaching and theological reflection.

6. ECUMENICAL

Vatican II acknowledged the ecclesial reality of other Christian churches, the presence of the Spirit to their members, and the grace-inspired character of their lives. It encouraged ecumenical dialogue and work and relaxed its discipline on common worship. Pointedly it stated: "Nor should we forget that whatever is wrought by the grace of the Holy Spirit in the hearts of our separated brethren can contribute to our own edification."[31]

The Council took this position with utter seriousness: "In fidelity to conscience, Christians are joined with the rest of men in the search for truth, and for the genuine solution to the numerous problems which arise in the life of individuals and from social relationships."[32]

In our time, one would think that ecumenism in moral discourse would be a given. Yet let me share a sneaking suspicion: ecumenical procedure is honored *except where the Holy See has taken an authoritative position in the past*. In those areas—and we all know what they are—consultants are chosen only if and because they agree with past formulations. Others, even and especially Catholics, are positively excluded. That this practice is a threat to ecumenical dialogue is clear. It is also clear that threats to such dialogue are threats to the church's credibility as well as its growth in understanding and witness.

That is why I dream of a moral theology by the year 2000 that is truly ecumenical.

7. INDUCTIVE IN METHOD

Inductive method follows from the personalism I noted above. Whether our actions or policies are supportive of persons or detrimental to them cannot be deduced from general principles. It takes time and experience. And the church must have the patience to provide for this maturation process.

In the decades prior to Vatican II, a much more deductive approach was in evidence. This is clear in the gradual transformation of social teaching in the church. As the Jesuit editors of *Civiltà cattolica* point out, the church's social teaching evolved through stages.[33] *Rerum novarum* represents the first stage, a stage dominated by "Christian philosophy" and a "rigidly deductive" method. This method had two shortcomings. First, it left no room for the relevance of the sciences (economics, sociology, political science). Second, and as a consequence, doctrinal elaboration was seen as an exclusively hierarchical task, lay persons being merely "faithful executors."

The second stage covers the pontificates of Pius XI and Pius XII and may be called the stage of "social doctrine." *Quadragesimo anno* used this term for the first time. It referred to an organic corpus of universal principles still rigidly deduced from social ethics. However, a greater emphasis on the historical moment and applications of principles to practice marked the beginnings of a reevaluation of the place of lay persons in the process.

The third stage began with John XXIII. John moved from the deductive to the inductive method, his point of departure being the "historical moment," to be viewed in light of the gospel. This move led to a complete reevaluation of the place of lay persons vis-à-vis social teaching, a reevaluation completed by Vatican II. The laity do not simply apply the church's social teaching; they must share in its very construction.

This development is an interesting phenomenon. One thing seems clear: a similar development has not occurred in all areas of Catholic moral theology—for instance, familial and sexual morality. If a clearly deductive method, one that left little room for the sciences and lay experience, prevailed in the elaboration of social teaching, it is reasonable to think that the same thing occurred in familial and sexual morality. And if the methodology of social teaching has evolved since John XXIII, it is reasonable to think that the same thing ought to happen in all areas of church teaching. But, as of now, it has not, and the inductive method remains part of my dream.

8. PLURALISTIC

There is something in the Catholic spirit that seems to feel the need for absolute agreement and conformity, even to the most detailed applications of moral principles. I think I know what that "something" is. It is a past authoritative teaching and practice that thought it possible to dot every "i" and cross every "t" on very detailed matters and imposed such certainties in a quite forceful and vigorous way. Public questioning of such conclusions was simply out of the question. Such imposed uniformity created expectations about Catholic unity that were intolerant of pluralism. A rather noisy but tiny minority still believes, for example, that we cannot disagree about *in vitro* fertilization between husband and wife, or about withdrawing artificial nutrition and hydration from persistently vegetative patients without forfeiting our basic Catholic unity.

In the United States these attitudes are concretely symbolized in the case of Charles Curran. Curran has repeatedly stated that his differences with authoritative pronouncements have three characteristics: (1) They concern matters remote from the core of faith; (2) they are matters heavily dependent on support from human reason; and (3) they are involved in such complexity and specificity that logically we cannot claim absolute certitude in their regard.[34]

I do not want to rehearse this issue here. Nor do I want to promote pluralism. Pluralism in these matters is a fact, not a value. It is a fact that we should expect and peacefully accept, especially in a church second to none in its reliance on the presence of the Spirit to its members.

In the decade ahead moral problems are only going to get more complicated and severe. That is why I dream of a moral theology that can live humbly, happily, and holily amid a degree of pluralism, indeed can welcome it as the sine qua non of growth in understanding.

9. ASPIRATIONAL

Moral theology will continue to be concerned with practical problems and problem solving. And it should be. Rightfulness and wrongfulness of conduct, while secondary, remains important. But a too exclusive concern with it can diminish other extremely important aspects of morality.

To make this point, let me distinguish between an ethics of minimal duty and an ethics of aspiration. The former is by and large minimalist, concerned with the negative, with uniform standards and legislative sanctions. Of it we may say what John Courtney Murray said about the notion of natural law:

> It does not show the individual the way to sainthood, but only to manhood. It does not promise to transform society into the City of God on earth, but only to prescribe, for the purpose of law and social custom, that minimum of morality which must be observed by the members of a society, if the social environment is to be human and habitable.[35]

If I read the "signs of the times" correctly, there are many people who, while by no means denying the importance of the "human and habitable," want more. They want an ethics of aspiration—one that is demanding, positive, aesthetic, centered on who they may become. We see this desire in medicine as physicians grow bored and restive with the commercialization of their profession. "Life must have more to offer than that" one said to me. We see it in business people who are sick and tired of a climate that makes profit not only a requirement but an obsession and forgets that there are stakeholders other than stockholders. We see it in educators, attorneys, and even ministers who feel that a merely functional or sacramental description of their challenges diminishes them.

In a word, then, the moral theology of the year 2000 will, I hope, pay much more attention to the "3 a.m. questions," the types of concerns we have as we hover between sleep and wakefulness. These questions are not the neon quandaries of ethics anthologies or the details of tomorrow's schedule. They are questions of guilt, personal integrity, of what my life is becoming, of God in my life, of genuine love, of mortality. They are aspirational questions. They are more invitational than obligational.

10. SPECIALIST

Here I can be mercifully brief. The day of the omnicompetent moral theologian is gone. Every aspect of life has its specialists. People spend professional lifetimes becoming experts in the oddest specialties: snail darters, the duodenum, rocketry, riverbed composition, childbearing in Tibet, computer software, and so on. McNeil-Lehrer regularly parade them before us.

My single and unsensational point is that if moral theology in the year 2000 is to be truly influential and a leaven for contemporary life, it must have thoroughly trained specialists who can mingle as equals in a world of specialists. Our theology will not influence medicine unless our theologians are medically knowledgeable and sophisticated. Much the same is true of law, business, economics, and other areas of human life.

What this means seems obvious: a severe limitation on what any one theologian undertakes to do and be. Daniel Callahan is what he is today in the world of bioethics because he limited himself and became credibly capable of challenging people on their own turf, and therefore of enlivening a whole discipline. The same is true of Bryan Hehir in foreign and strategic affairs.

In summary, then, I dream of a moral theology that is

1. Christocentric and anchored in charity (vs. one one-sidedly philosophical).
2. Universalizing in its appeal (vs. one narrowly sectarian).
3. With appropriate subsidiarity (vs. overcentralization).
4. Personalist (vs. excessively biologistic).
5. Modest and tentative (vs. "infallibilistic").
6. Ecumenical (vs. exclusively parochial and Roman).
7. Inductive (vs. abstractly deductive in method).
8. Pluralistic (vs. a universal conformism).
9. Aspirational (vs. minimalistic).
10. Specialistic (vs. omnicompetent).

What will it take to get such a theology? The very question supposes that we are not there yet, indeed are far from it. I have no solutions-by-microwave. But one idea returns persistently in my dream. It is the fact that in a world church in which changes are so dramatic and frequent, an ecumenical council only every one hundred years is, well, quite literally medieval. What councils meeting every ten years (I propose such a schedule here) might do to see that our structures truly reflect a world church is the matter of another dream. But I have no doubt that moral theology would be profoundly affected.

In the meantime, the best that our theologians can do is to toil humbly and courageously as if my reverie were a reality. In doing so they will hurry the day when it will be.

NOTES

1. Jaroslav Pelikan, *The Vindication of Tradition* (New Haven: Yale University Press, 1984), 58.

2. Peter Hebblethwaite, "Synod Dreams," *National Catholic Reporter*, 24 October 1980, 20.

3. Karl Rahner, "Dream of the Church," *Tablet* 235 (1981): 52-55.

4. St. Thomas Aquinas, *Summa Theologiae* I-II.91.a2. "Fit providentiae particeps, sibi ipsi et aliis providens."

5. Cited in Eugene Kennedy's *Re-Imagining American Catholicism* (New York: Random House Vintage Books, 1985), 19.

6. Andrew M. Greeley, "Defection among Hispanics," *America* 159 (1988): 62.

7. John Mahoney, S.J., *The Making of Moral Theology* (Oxford: Clarendon Press, 1987).

8. Don Peppers, "Make Money, Have Fun, Be Ethical," *New York Times*, 24 July 1988, III,3:1.

9. Enrico Chiavacci, "The Grounding for the Moral Norm in Contemporary Theological Reflection," in *Readings in Moral Theology 2*, ed. Charles E. Curran and Richard A. McCormick, S.J. (Ramsey, New Jersey: Paulist, 1980), 291-292.

10. Joseph Sittler, *The Structure of Christian Ethics* (Baton Rouge: Louisiana State University Press, 1958), 50-51.

11. John Courtney Murray, *We Hold These Truths* (Kansas City: Sheed & Ward, 1960), 296.

12. Karl Rahner, S.J., "A Basic Interpretation of Vatican II," *Theological Studies* 40 (1979): 716-727.

13. Walter M. Abbot, ed., *Documents of Vatican II* (New York: Association Press, 1966), 209 Hereafter, *Documents*.

14. *Documents*, 240.

15. Stanley Hauerwas, "The Demands of a Truthful Story: Ethics and the Pastoral Task," *Chicago Studies* 21(1982): 59-71.

16. John H. Yoder, "The Hermeneutics of Peoplehood: A Protestant Perspective on Practical Moral Reasoning," *Journal of Religious Ethics* 10 (1982): 40-67 at 63.

17. "The Hermeneutics of Peoplehood," 64.

18. Roger L. Shinn, "Homosexuality: Christian Conviction and Inquiry," in Ralph W. Weltge, ed., *The Same Sex* (Philadelphia: Pilgrim Press, 1969), 43-54 at 51.

19. Pius XI, *Quadragesimo anno*, para 79, 80 in Terence P. McLaughlin, ed., *The Church and the Reconstruction of the Modern World: The Social Encyclicals of Pope Pius XI* (Garden City: Doubleday-Image, 1957), 246-247.

20. *Documents*, 199, footnote 2.

21. *Documents*, 244.

22. *Documents*, 232.

23. *The Challenge of Peace* (Washington, D.C.: United States Catholic Conference, 1983), 4.

24. *Documents*, 244.

25. Murray, *We Hold These Truths*, 296.

26. Franciscus Hürth, S.J., "*La fécondation artificielle: Sa valuer morale et juridique*," *Nouvelle revue théologique* 68 (1946): 402-426 at 416.

27. John C. Ford, S.J., and Gerald Kelly, S.J., *Contemporary Moral Theology: Marriage Questions* (Westminster, Maryland: Newman, 1963), 288.

28. Louis Janssens, "Artificial Insemination: Ethical Considerations," *Louvain Studies* 8 (1980): 3-29 at 24.

29. Rahner, as in note 3.

30. Congregation for the Doctrine of the Faith, *Inner insigniores* in Austin Flannery, ed., *Vatican Council II More Postconciliar Documents* (Northport, New York: Costello Publishing Co., 1982), 338.

31. *Documents*, 349.

32. *Documents*, 214.

33. "Dalla 'Rerum novarum' ad oggi," *Civiltà cattolica* 132 (1981): 345-357.

34. Charles E. Curran, "Public Dissent in the Church," *Origins* 16 (1986): 178-84 at 181-182.

35. Murray, *We Hold These Truths*, 297.

JOHN T. NOONAN, JR.

3

The Metaphors of Morals

Good is brightness, evil darkness . . .
According to the nature of our bodies, of our language.[1]

"High aims and low conduct." "A straight line or a crooked path."
"Right thinking or sinister purpose." "Clean hands or dirty hands."
Incurably, the language of morals is metaphoric. Perhaps the most
popular of moral and legal ways of expressing a judgment today is
through the ambiguous, generally unanalyzed metaphor of balance. Is
a balanced judgment one in which a person has weighed values as
scales weigh quantities, or is it a judgment that has reached a state of
functional fitness akin to biological well-being? Whichever the understanding, "balanced" is not an immediate description of a mind but an
evocation of a tangible equilibrium.

Metaphors, Benjamin Cardozo tells us, "are to be narrowly
watched, for starting as devices to liberate thought, they end often by
enslaving it." Even more darkly, Learned Hand, citing Cardozo,
declares, "Much of the metaphor in the books merely impedes discourse . . .; here, as elsewhere, it is ordinarily a symptom of confused
thinking." [2]

The great metaphors of Western morals offer histories that confirm these somber judgments. Yet language and human limitations
compel us to use the tools at hand, images among them; and the three
metaphoric notions I propose to examine here have not only confused
and enslaved; they have liberated and enlightened. They have func-
tioned programmatically to point to human characteristics that make
moral discourse possible and at times profitable. The visual or spatial
or anatomical or hygienic images I recalled at the start have all had the
very useful function of classifying, of separating, of proclaiming a difference between the good and the bad. The metaphors have drama-
tized the difference that is at the center of moral judgment. The three
powerful and recurrent metaphors I shall look at in more detail are not
only dramatic but foundational. I denominate these notions "metaphors"—someone else might call them ideas or concepts—because

35

they embody images, suggest a physical dimension, and do no more than capture the likeness of one aspect of what they purport to denote or describe.

NATURE

I begin with "Nature"—the image of a reality possessed of an origin, a solidity, and a stability independent of human intervention; a sign for what does not depend on human desire or design; and because of these special characteristics, endowed with an authority that is normative for human conduct. So in Aristotle's ethics for Nichomacus, the natural is contrasted with the legal—the natural in Aristotle's cautious way being recognized as not utterly unchangeable but as a good deal more constant than such matters of human agreement as a prescribed penalty or propitiation.[3] The insinuation—it is perhaps in the master himself not stronger—is that the natural is the measure of the conventional. In the famous passage in the *Politics* on usury, the breeding of money is said to be unnatural. It appears to be a criticism.

In the Stoics, the insinuation has become insistence: nature is the key, especially in the area of sex. "As the eye is to see, so the genitalia are to generate"—the sentence is delivered with the force of an axiom. It claims the authority of an insight into anthropology undisturbed by human arbitrariness: it asserts that this is the way things are. Adopted by Augustine, the Stoic notion of nature is the bedrock of Western sexual morals as articulated, inculcated, and enforced for over 1,500 years. The "sin against nature" becomes in the hands of Christian moralists a comprehensive category within which can fall contraception, *coitus interruptus*, anal intercourse, oral intercourse, masturbation, uncustomary sexual positions, and unisexual sex. The category of unnatural is not only a catchall for a variety of acts; the category also provides the clue as to why the acts are condemned: they are *contra naturam*.[4]

Parallel to the exposition of the ethics of sex runs the exposition of the ethics of money. The usury prohibition is central to the economic ethics of the West from Ambrose of Milan in the fourth century to Alfonso de' Liguori in the eighteenth. In the *Inferno* this colloquy occurs between Dante and Virgil:

> *"Go back a little," I said,*
> *"Where you said that*
> *Usury offends divine goodness, and*
> *Untie the knot."*[5]

"Knot" implies that the problem is difficult, without an obvious solution. The knot is untied by Philosophy, which indicates that man must follow nature or at least the art that tracks nature. Such, according to the poem, is the teaching of Aristotle's *Physics* on nature; such is the teaching of Genesis. The usurer, however, "takes another way." He acts contrary to the nature of the universe and the creator of the universe. The sin is a form of violence against God, blaspheming him and despising Nature and her goodness. Usurers, accordingly, reside in lower Hell, in the Seventh Circle, from which arises "a horrible excess of stink." They are lumped with the homosexuals in a line that treats as parallel Sodom, the city renowned for homosexual lusts, and Cahors, the Provencal town notorious for its moneylenders:

> *The smallest ring seals with its mark*
> *Both Sodom and Cahors.*[6]

The recurrent appeal to nature still reverberates in the poetry of Ezra Pound, the last man in the West to write with passion on the subject:

> *Usura slayeth the child in the womb*
> *It stayeth the young man's courting*
> *It hath brought palsey to bed, lyeth*
> *between the young bride and her bridegroom*
> > *Contra Naturam*
> *They have brought whores for Eleusis*
> *Corpses set to banquet*
> *at behest of usura.*[7]

Usury is against nature: Pound invokes Aristotle, Ambrose, Thomas, the tradition of Western morals. But what a strange nature is being invoked!

The argument depends on determinations made by civil legislation and on assumptions about the purpose of this legislation. Money, Aristotle acknowledges, was invented by human beings as a measure of value; its very name *nomisma* indicates that it is a matter of convention.[8] Money, Aristotle assumes, has this single purpose of measuring value. To use money for other purposes, according to his scholastic successors, is to depart from the purpose for which money was created. But why is it against the nature of things to adapt a human invention to a second purpose? "Against nature" in this argument against usury really means "against legal purpose." Instead of being in contrast to conventional legal rules, "nature" depends on them. Nothing could illustrate more forcefully the hypnotic force of the image. The most artificial of human inventions has been invested with the properties of the universe beyond human manipulation. The inversion is so complete that those who invoked it for two thousand years never noticed.

So much the worse for metaphor you may conclude. But the positive side of the balance has not been considered. The notion of Nature, first and fundamentally, announced that what was good or bad did not depend entirely on what any individual wanted: there was a norm in some way objective; moral anarchism was rejected. Second, and equally fundamental, Nature proclaimed a comparability of human beings that did not depend on status, power, wealth, religion, or race. Nature was commitment to human equality, to the likeness that human beings share independently of all social determinations. Third, and surely equally basic, Nature was proclamation that human morals are rooted in this earth, that what is right for human beings is to be found in their capacities, satisfactions, and limits.

The corollaries of these propositions were several. A ruler, whether secular or ecclesiastical, would act wrongly if he violated the laws of nature. A ruler, whether secular or ecclesiastical, could not dispense from the laws of nature. Rightness or wrongness, in at least some matters, did not depend on the ruler's will. Individual human beings were furnished with a moral claim to inviolability in some ways. Against the arbitrariness of power, there was an argument.[9]

"Nature" was, moreover, a program of investigation. At first the investigators did not push far, were perfunctory. But as long as the issue turned on what was natural, the natural could be explored. Even the paradoxical use of "Nature" to analyze the lending of money, a legal invention, led to a vast investigation of the devices of commerce and credit, an intellectual enterprise that would not have been undertaken without the invitation "Nature" offered.[10] And beyond investigation, the nonvolitional norm provided by Nature offered the possibility of control. That unmanipulable Nature should afford the basis for human design was another paradox, of course, but a paradox implicit in the invocation of Nature as norm. In the economic case, for example, the discovery of what was natural offered the prospect of controlling economic forces. A whole immense side of social life, once left to the play of unanalyzed factors, was visualized as susceptible to examination, rationalization, and control.[11]

If you press further and ask what the practical payoff of Nature was, I would answer, first that in this matter as in all accounts of social causes, it is difficult to isolate the effect of key variables—one can only make an informed estimate; and second, in our own case, Nature was the key image in the single most momentous transformation of our society.

Committed by the Declaration of Independence to a belief in natural rights, and by the Constitution to the enforcement of slavery, no nation ever experienced more acutely in its national leadership the conflict between moral ideal and existing law. "May not the miserable African ask," exclaimed Justice Story in Boston, "Am I not a man and a brother?"[12] Slaveholding-Chief Justice Marshall could write that every person had a natural right to the fruits of his labor. A necessary result of this admission "seemed to be" that no person had a right to deprive another of the fruits of his labor by making him his slave.[13] With consciences such as these at the top of the legal edifice of the Union, the slavery-enforcing Union could not survive when, in the generation following Marshall, preachers such as Parker declared slavery to be against "an ordinance of nature," and senators such as Seward said, "If the Constitution recognized property in slaves, it would suffice to say this constitutional recognition must be void because it is repugnant to the law of nature and of nations."[14]

RECIPROCITY

I turn to a second metaphor more modern in fashion but also ancient and recurrent—Reciprocity. Reciprocity is an image of equality in exchange. It wears the character of a physical law, as though one force must generate a reaction of equal force. "Do *ut des*," as Roman law neatly expresses it: "I give that you may give." The return is to be equal. Justice in contracts, Aristotle assures us, is arithmetical, not proportional: 2 is exchanged for 2 in a fair contract.[15] Physical equality is particularly palpable in the reciprocity sought in punishment. "Eye for eye, tooth for tooth, hand for hand, foot for foot" (Exod 21:24). "The Pythagoreans," Aristotle adds, "defined justice absolutely as retaliation."[16] Poetic justice is like that: Joseph's brothers enslave an innocent and end as his prisoners (Gen 37:28, Gen 42:16). The rule of Rhadamanthus, the judge of Hades, is this:

> As a man's action, so his fate.
> Thus justice is true and straight.[17]

Shakespeare, in what is not quite the last word of *Measure for Measure*, recalls the rule in the Duke's judgment:

> "An Angelo for Claudio! death for death!"
> Haste still pays haste, and leisure answers leisure
> Like doth quit like, and Measure still for Measure.[18]

The objective orderliness, the tangible fairness of equality of exchange, whether the exchange be voluntary or involuntary, exerts a powerful appeal on all imaginations. For example, in that triumphant expression of American theology, the Second Inaugural Address, Abraham Lincoln, speaking to the hearts of his countrymen, conceives of the Civil War continuing "until every drop of blood drawn by the lash shall be paid for by the sword."[19] The payment in blood is to be exact. Arithmetic prevails.

The image is merely a metaphor. Apart from the simplest cases, equality of exchange is impossible. In contracts, no one does business by exchanging identical objects: the fair exchange is of objects estimated to be proportionate to each other; physical equivalence disappears with the use of money. In torts, if a negligent driver costs you your arm, you cannot take his. In criminal law, there are only a few physical injuries avengeable by infliction of the same injury. A traitor is not punished by betrayal; a perjurer is not punished by being lied about. The rule of criminal justice cannot be equality; the just response is merely proportionate.

The image of Reciprocity, like that of Nature, has thus been extended beyond its limits. Making the punishment fit the crime is simple if one believes one is eliminating a negative force by a positive force of the same magnitude. A judgment of proportion is far more difficult. No easy arithmetic permits the proportion to be calculated. The dominance of the image of Reciprocity in notions of the criminal law as retaliative or restorative has hindered a candid approach to the purposes of punishment.

In many societies, Reciprocity has often obscured the need for nonreciprocal relationships apart from the family. In such societies, one approaches a powerful stranger with a gift in hand if one wants a peaceful and benevolent response. The bearer of gifts imposes a burden of return on the recipient. Such was the rule in the ancient Near East.[20] Such was the rule—so a modern anthropologist reports— among Melanesians, Papuans, and Indians of northwest America.[21] To Marcel Mauss, the modern anthropologist, Reciprocity is the key to morality; it is not *a* rule, but *the* rule of life. "There is," he writes, apparently normatively as well as descriptively, "no other morality, no other economy, no other social practice."[22]

Enslavement of this sort to equality in exchange prevents perception of evil in Reciprocity. Strikingly, anthropologists tend not to see any reciprocities as bad; they apparently find a concept of bad Reciprocity missing in their subjects. But cultures in the Western tradition have perceived that Reciprocity is sometimes wrong—most notably when it is an exchange between a litigant and a judge; by extension, when it is an exchange between a suppliant for governmental favor and an official or even an exchange between a campaign contributor and a legislator. The classic languages had no unambiguous term for what was offered in these illicit exchanges.

Shohadh in Hebrew, doron in Greek, munus in Latin were applied indifferently to gifts in good and bad exchanges. English in the sixteenth century crystallized the social disapproval of bad reciprocities in the word "bribe."[23] The linguistic shift was a significant escape from the spell of Reciprocity as the only rule of life. The spell lingers in the strong popular sense—captured for example in Measure for Measure—that a double-crossing bribetaker—one who does not reciprocate his bribe—is worse than a bribetaker who delivers.[24] Such double-dealing was a fault of Francis Bacon as a judge and contributed to his criminal conviction.[25] But the healthy expression of an antibribery ethic has demonstrated that Reciprocity no longer rules unchallenged.

Equality in exchange was a misleading metaphor. What benefits did the image of Reciprocity confer? I identify three. First, Reciprocity implicitly assumes a likeness between the persons making the exchange. Equality is called for because the exchangers are in some way equal. If they were of a totally different species, no reciprocities would be possible. Like Nature, Reciprocity points to human equality.

Second, Reciprocity provides a clue to proportionateness in judgment. Moving beyond retaliation in punishment, it invites the punisher to put himself in the place of the one punished—Reciprocity of this sort is, in Shakespeare's phrase, "a kind of medicine" for authority.[26] If what is done would be fair to do for the same offense committed by the one exercising authority, the penalty is proportionate.

Third, Reciprocity becomes a law of generosity. At the level of alms to the needy, the perception is as old as the kingdom of Lagash in 2400 B.C., that if the king helps the poor, the gods will repay the king.[27] The theme is emphatic in the New Testament. Invite the poor, the weak, the lame to supper and "it will be repaid to you in the resurrection of the just" (Luke 14:13-14). Beyond physical aid, Reciprocity is stated as the rule of spiritual life: "You have received freely. Give freely" (Matt 10:8). Transformed from grudging calculation of quantity, Reciprocity can no longer corrupt. As Measure for Measure triumphantly concludes, an act of forgiveness wins forgiveness.[28] In this way, the iron law of death for death is broken. Reciprocity, transformed, becomes the invitation of man proposed to God: "Forgive our debts as we have forgiven our debtors" (Matt 6:12).

THE LAST JUDGMENT

Reciprocity, plain and simple, measures morality as though physical forces were being gauged. "Nature" leans on what is common to

human beings and other animals. A third metaphor that has been cru-
cial for moral thought has been that of the Last Judgment—a judgment
at which all masks are removed, all truth revealed, all wrongs righted,
and all good acts rewarded. For example, in the *Book of the Dead* of the
Egyptian noble Ani, circa 1300 B.C., the heart of Ani is depicted as it is
weighed against a feather, a hieroglyph signifying Truth or Justice. The
balance must be exact for Ani to pass beyond the Judgment Hall.[29] In
the tale that rounds out Plato's *Republic*, judges sentence the dead to
ascend on the right or to descend on the left, and the penalty for an evil
deed is at least tenfold with some great tyrants being tortured by
thorns and scourging in perpetuity, proportionality giving way to a
sense that some crimes are beyond redemption, forgiveness, expiation,
or ultimate amnesty.[30] Near the climax of the Gospel of Matthew, the
Son of Man, accompanied by angels, sits on a throne of glory, separating the nations as a shepherd separates sheep from goats, welcoming
the charitable on his right into his kingdom, and dispatching the
uncharitable on his left into everlasting fire (Matt 25:31-46).

All of these tableaux present visual images of great power. They
have tortured minds that have taken them as paintings of a possible
destiny. Take, for example, this passage from Innocent III's *The Misery
of the Human Condition*, adopted wholesale in a wholly secular work,
The Laws and Customs of England, the greatest treatise on English law
before Blackstone:

> There will be weeping and gnashing of teeth, groans and moans,
> cries and sighs and agony, shrieking and screeching, shaking and
> shuddering, suffering and travailing, fire and stink, darkness and
> dread, bitterness and boisterousness, ruin and waste, distress and
> dejection, oblivion and disorder, torturings and piercings, tor-
> ments and terrors, hunger and thirst, frigidity and boiling heat,
> brimstone and fire burning forever and ever.[31]

The passage is, in lieu of more secular deterrents, intended to persuade
the judges of thirteenth century England not to accept bribes. The *ad
terrorem* intention is evident. The terror deflects attention from the
bribetaker's vice to the rich resources of the Punisher.

The Matthean image is more balanced. The dramatic details of
the scene are subordinate to the central metaphor of moral judgment.
Part of the program implied in the metaphor is like that contained in
Nature and Reciprocity: human beings are equal, all are judged, and all
are judged by the same criteria. Our mass of petty distinctions—even
gender and age—disappears. Part of the program is pointed at the
individual person as much as at an egalitarian community. Moral judg-

ment, the metaphor proclaims, is desirable—that is, good and evil are done; they are done by choice; they are worth distinguishing; moral judgment is a divine activity. Finally, the program focuses on individual responsibility. Moral judgment, it says, may be made of a person; that is, an identity prevails so that a person is judged not for isolated acts but on a course of life. In the end, each person is accountable for what he or she becomes.

This metaphor does not come from animal life; it does not come from physics. This metaphor draws on the human practice of judging offenders against governments. It is not an image, however, of any real court. Even in the ancient Near East, judges did not, like shepherds, size up defendants with a glance. The judgment is effected not only without the aid of advocates or accusers (unlike human judgments), but is also sure, undeceived, and ultimate. What is perhaps most remarkable is that the Divine Judge—even the Christian Judge, who has been grievously offended by sin—is implicitly assumed to be impartial. The Judge is not avenging wrongs done to the Judge. The Judge is determining the nature, at the end, of each person before him. The metaphor is a metaphor for moral judgment itself. The central operation of moral thought, critical evaluation, is symbolized and projected in the form of the divine activity. The model of moral judgment is pictured as the impartial discernment of moral realities.

The most famous literary development of the theme of the Last Judgment is Dante's; the most famous painting, Michelangelo's in the Sistine Chapel. Each, properly understood, is faithful to the central metaphor. Dante's sinners are engaged in activities symbolic of their sin: the lustful, for example, move in a ceaseless whirl; the bribetakers are coated with sticky pitch.[32] In Michelangelo, Leo Steinberg has persuasively argued, there are no damned souls. Only allegorical vices are eternally punished.[33]

Much of what I have pointed to may confirm Cardozo on the enslaving effect of metaphor and Hand on metaphor as a symptom of confusion. One may long for Thrasymachus's standard of clear and precise definitions, such as his definition that justice is the interest of the stronger,[34] or even prefer Quine's *Quiddities* where the great logician throws up his hands and says that he knows that "gratuitous killing" is proscribed but beyond "that salient marker" are only "unchartered moral wastes."[35]

But the business of making morals goes on even if cynics or skeptics opt out; law is impossible without morals; and in their manufacture (not out of whole cloth) metaphors are magnifiers as well as mystifiers. Nature, a metaphor, invited rational investigation of one area, sex, hitherto locked in custom, and examination of another area, economics, hitherto utterly unexplored. And Nature provided a moral claim against the arbitrariness of power. Reciprocity, a metaphor for self-interested exchange, opened the way to a new generosity of the spirit where gift led to giving and the measure matching measure was forgiving in exchange for forgiveness. The Last Judgment, a metaphor extended almost to allegory, made central the critical place in the moral enterprise of impartial self-examination and comprehensive and unsparing self-assessment. I have prescinded from the truth of the metaphors. But none of these metaphors would have worked at all if it had been completely arbitrary, if there had not been a response in human experience, if it were not true that human beings have purposes that are not entirely malleable; that there is a rhythm in human interaction that produces equivalences, that in some sense, to someone—ourselves or another—we are accountable, and that that accountability holds promise.

NOTES

1. Czelaw Milosz, "One More Day," in Milosz, *Unattainable Earth* (New York: Ecco Press, 1986), 34.

2. Berkey v. Third Ave. Ry Co. 244 N.Y. 84,94; 155 N.E. 58,61 (1926) (per Cardozo, C.J.); Kingston Dry Dock Co. v. Lake Champlain Transportation Co. 31 F.2d 265,267 (2d Cir. 1919) (per Hand, J.).

3. Aristotle, *Nichomachean Ethics*, trans. J.E.C. Welldon (1902) 5.7.

4. See John T. Noonan, Jr., *Contraception: A History of Its Treatment by the Catholic Theologians and Canonists* (Cambridge: Harvard University Press, 1965), 75, 78, 172-173, 187-188, 223-226.

5. Dante, *La Divina Commedia: Inferno* 11.94-95.

6. *Inferno* 11.50.

7. Ezra Pound, *Cantos* 45.230-40.

8. *Nichomachean Ethics,* 5.5.

9. See Noonan, "Tokos and Atokion: An Examination of Natural Law Reasoning Against Usury and Against Contraception," *Natural Law Forum* 10 (1965).

10. Ibid.

11. See John T. Noonan, Jr., *The Scholastic Analysis of Usury* (Cambridge: Harvard University Press, 1957).

12. See Story, J. in La Jeune Eugenie, 26 F. Cas. 832 (1822).

13. Marshall, C.J. in The Antelope, 10 Wheat. 66, 120 (1825).

14. See Theodore Parker, "Mr. Webster's Speech," Parker, *Works* 3, 37; William Seward, Speech, Cong. Globe, App., 11 March 1850, 264.

15. *Nichomachean Ethics,* 5.4.

16. Ibid., 5.5.

17. Ibid.

18. William Shakespeare, *Measure for Measure*, act 5, scene 1.

19. Abraham Lincoln, Second Inaugural Address, *Collected Works*, ed. Roy P. Basler (New Brunswick: Rutgers University Press, 1953) 8, 333.

20. John T. Noonan, Jr., *Bribes* (New York: Macmillan, 1984), 7-14.

21. Marcel Mauss, *Essai sur le don: Forme et raison de l'échange dans les sociétes archa* (Paris: Presses Universitaires, 1968), 153.

22. Ibid., 277-279. As Claude Levi-Strauss remarks in his preface to the 1968 edition of Mauss' essay, originally published in 1925, Mauss "had assigned to ethnology an essential end, to contribute to the enlargement of human reason." Ibid., vi. The celebration of the reciprocity created by gift fulfilled this function by pointing to this way to peace.

23. *Bribes*, 315.

24. *Measure for Measure*, act 5.

25. *Bribes*, 356.

26. *Measure for Measure*, act 2, scene 2.

27. F. Charles Fenshaw, "Widow, Orphan, and the Poor in Ancient Near Eastern Legal and Wisdom Literature," *Journal of Near Eastern Studies* 21 (1962): 130.

28. *Measure for Measure*, act 5.

29. *The Book of the Dead—the Papyrus of Ani*, ed. E.A. Wallis Budge (London: The Medici Society, 1913), Plates 1-4.

30. Plato, *Republic*, 10.

31. Henri de Bracton, *De legibus et consuetudinibus Angliae*, ed. Samuel E. Thorne (Cambridge: Harvard University Press, 1977) 2, 21-22.

32. *Inferno*, canto 21.

33. Leo Steinberg, "Michelangelo's *Last Judgment* as Merciful Heresy," *Art in America* (November/December 1975): 53.

34. *Republic* 1.12.

35. William V. Quine, *Quiddities* (Cambridge: Harvard University Press, 1987), 5.

4

Secular Morality and Sacred Obligation

UNITY OF RELIGION AND MORALITY

Before discussing religion and morality as two entirely distinct subjects, we ought to remind ourselves of their original unity. In an archaic
society this unity is taken for granted. In Emile Durkheim's words:

> It has been said that primitive peoples had no morality. That was
> an historical error. There is no people without its morality. How-
> ever, the morality of undeveloped societies is not ours. What
> characterizes them is that they are essentially religious. By that, I
> mean that the most numerous and important duties are not the
> duties of man toward other men, but of man toward his gods.[1]

Morality as a separate branch of learning that deals with obligations
distinct from rituals, customs, class, or tribal orders, never existed in
most societies. *Ethics*, as its etymology indicates, originally referred to
what people actually do, because they feel that they ought to do it for
whatever reason. Within that same universal perspective, virtue (*arete*
for Plato and Aristotle) still means "excellence" in any field. Aristotle
(followed by Saint Thomas) ranks intellectual virtues on a par with
moral ones. For him, the term "ethical" certainly does not have the
purely deontological meaning that we have come to attach to it.

MacIntyre translates *ethikos* as "pertaining to character" and that
is how it made its way into the Latin *moralis*.[2] The idea of a secular
"morality" comprehending duties that apply to atheists and believers
does not seem to have been current before the later part of the seven-
teenth century. The French philosopher Pierre Bayle may well have
been the first to defend it in principle.

Limiting the discussion to our own tradition we find that three of
antiquity's major philosophers set up different moral models all of

which served Christians in elaborating a morality intrinsically dependent on their religion. The first model appears in Plato, the second in Aristotle, the third in Stoic philosophy. For Plato, the idea of the Good, by its very beauty, attracts and inspires the highest and noblest part of the soul. The purpose of life is to approach that ideal with all our powers until it takes full possession of us. Iris Murdoch put it well:

> One might say that true morality is a sort of mysticism, having its source in an austere and unconsoled love of the Good. When Plato wants to explain good, he uses the image of the sun. The moral pilgrim emerges from the cave and begins to see the real world in the light of the sun, and, last of all, is able to look at the sun itself.[3]

This vision certainly differs from Kant's understanding of morality.

Plato's vision passed, almost unchanged, to Augustine, the most influential Latin Father. Through him, it became the model of a divine attraction that lifts the mind beyond all finite desires, toward a divine ideal. In Augustine's "irrequietum est cor nostrum donec requiescat in te Domine" still resounds the voice of Plato's Eros. But he strengthens the appeal of the Good by identifying it with a Person.

With Aristotle we enter, of course, a wholly different world, yet not as different as we tend to think. In his early *Protreptikos*, Aristotle echoed the language of his master: "Who has even once contemplated the divine must wonder whether anything is great and durable in human reality." The norm of action, if we may believe the *Eudemian Ethics* to reflect Aristotle's own theory, consists in the contemplation of God. There are perhaps two moral ideals in the *Nicomachean Ethics*, and it is by no means clear how they are related. Is the tenth book, which presents contemplation as the supreme good, fully compatible with the rest of the work, which promotes more active and political virtues? At any rate, Aristotle's *theoria* consists of intellectual activity, not of devotional contemplation. The religious act of surrender to God has little to do with it.

In the main part of the *Nicomachean Ethics*, perfection consists in what we would probably call self-actualization. Since the highest human capacity is reason, it is by actualizing reason that a person reaches the highest perfection. Happiness, the subjective and agreeable awareness of this objective state of well-being, follows from it. The idea of a moral *obligation*, as Stoics or Christians understood it, appears to be absent. In fact, human action is not measured by any transcendent norm, but by experience alone.

Despite this apparently "secular" view, Aristotle's theory served as a basis for a second model of a religiously inspired morality. As interpreted by St. Thomas, the pursuit of personal perfection and happiness implies in fact the quest for an absolute Good: finite goodness partakes of the total good of a divine absolute. We detect a Platonic slant in this reading of Aristotelian ethics. Nevertheless, the accent on *personal* perfection sufficiently distinguishes it from Plato's *ec-static* ideal to justify considering it a different model.

The third classical model emerges with the Stoa: it includes a transcendent obligation. Nothing illustrates it more directly than the following fragment from Epictetus's *Diatribes*, describing how the good person ought to be able to address God at the moment of death:

> The faculties which I received from you to enable me to under-stand your governance and to follow it, these I have not neglected; I have not dishonored You as far as in me lay. Behold how I have dealt with my senses, behold how I have dealt with my preconceptions. Have I ever blamed You? . . . For that You begot me I am grateful; for what You have given I am grateful also. The length of time for which I have had the use of Your gifts is enough for me. Take them back again and assign them to what place You will, for they were all yours, and You gave them to me.[4]

Here the religious connotation is overt, and Christian writers found in the Stoic concept a direct support for their position that the moral obligation derives, in fact, from a divine command. It initiated a long line of religious interpretations of the concept of duty that culminate in Newman's declaration that the voice of conscience is the voice of God. Since the idea of obligation dominates ethics in the modern age, most of the controversy centers around this third model. It is from that perspective that in the next section I shall consider the question: Does morality depend on religion?

LOSS OF RELIGION AND MORAL DECLINE

At least in the past, each society possessed its own code of behavior, and since religion in archaic and traditional societies was all-comprehensive, that code reflected the dominant religious vision. It is to be expected, then, that any decline of the founding religion will entail a decline of its specific code of morals. But does such a decline mean more than a *temporary* crisis, caused by the transition from one code to another? Certain accepted values suffer from it. But as the secular observer might say, to rid a society of its exclusive religious code is a major step forward in the direction of a universal morality. Is the particularity of each religion and of the moral code it introduces not the main source of dissent, unrest, and war in the world?

The believer will, of course, retort that the loss of religion signifies a substantial moral decline. Since the person's obligation to God forms an essential part of moral life, to abolish religious duties results in a truncated, incomplete moral code. But to an outsider, such an argument begs the question. It merely states that a religiously conceived morality requires a religious foundation. If we assume, as many of our contemporaries do, that public morality ought to be religiously neutral in a manner that enables people, despite ideological differences, to observe rules of justice and even of charity toward one another, the argument loses much of its power. Is it fair to call those who do not share our religious beliefs immoral? Fairness aside, to do so in a pluralistic society can only deepen our divisions and weaken the chance of an agreement on basic moral principles. Thus I shall take my stand on that neutral domain. If the case for a religious foundation cannot be made here, it will fail to convince those who are not yet a priori convinced. If we abandon this religiously neutral position, the common ground for a moral discussion vanishes altogether.

Another issue related to an intrinsically religious view of morality needs to be clarified. If indeed, as we have assumed, much of our moral code has a religious origin, then, is not the agnostic in a Christian culture in fact living off religious capital? He certainly appears to be spending what he has not earned! If we all did so, the moral capital would gradually become depleted, for lack of new religious input. Standards would fall and inspiration dry up. But this objection also, though historically correct about the religious origins of morality, misses the point of the contemporary argument. The question concerns not origins—many agnostics would happily concede that we owe the precept to love our neighbor to the Sermon on the Mount—but whether generally acceptable moral norms, *in whatever way introduced*, can or cannot be sustained in a religiously neutral climate. Do they possess enough *substance* to maintain themselves without a religious authority? If not, they are not worth preserving. But if they do and continue to be accepted by nonbelievers, the moral content no longer needs the original religious support. The language of morals may in that respect be misleading. Religious believers tend to read more in it than is there. As the British philosopher W.G. MacLagen put it:

> It seems to me quite untrue to say, for instance, that the *substance* of our thought when we speak of the brotherhood of man neces-

sarily presupposes a conviction of the fatherhood of God, although it may be the case that this language would not naturally, or even could not properly, be used in the *expression* of our thought except in association with such a conviction.[5]

This brings us to the heart of the matter: Does the moral obligation presuppose *One* who obliges? We know how in his three *Critiques* Kant consistently denied that the presence of a moral imperative provided a proof of the existence of a divine lawgiver. Even in his later *Religion Within the Limits of Reason Alone*, Kant is unambiguous: "For its own sake morality does not need religion at all . . .; by virtue of pure practical reason it is self-sufficient."[6] In his *Opus Posthumum*, however, he appears to relent when asserting that the religious perception of all duties, in which he had claimed the essence of religion to consist, is not given *subsequently* to our perception of them as duties, but *in* and *with* the perception itself. "The categorical imperative of the command of duty is grounded in the idea of an *imperantis*, who is all-powerful and holds universal sway. This is the idea of God."[7]

The moral obligation would thereby become intrinsically religious and, as Norman Kemp Smith concluded, the categorical imperative, then, "leads directly to God, and affords surety of his reality."[8] One may, of course, dismiss this single observation which contradicts all that Kant had maintained through a lifetime of reflection, as the scribbling of a scholar in his doting years. But an impressive number of other thinkers—in the full vigor of their intellectual life—have lent support to Kant's conclusion. Thus, Hans Küng in *Does God Exist?* claims that no notion derived from human nature or from reason alone can ever be absolute. "Why should I observe these norms unconditionally? Why should I observe them even when they are completely at variance with my interests?"[9]

An absolute obligation can come only from an absolute Being. Similarly, Edouard Le Roy, Bergson's great disciple, wrote "Il y a un Absolu au fond de l'exigence morale: le reconnaître c'est affirmer Dieu déjà, de quelque nom qu'on le homme et quelque imparfaitement qu'on le conçoive."[10] Le Roy follows Kant in denying that the moral obligation is "deduced" from the religious affirmative: the two are perceived simultaneously. For English-speaking Christians, the idea of a religious foundation of morality is strongly connected with the name of John Henry Newman who described the voice of conscience as an authoritative "dictate" which threatens and promises, rewards and chastises, reminding us "that there is One to whom we are responsible, before whom we are ashamed, whose claims upon us we fear."[11]

Impressive testimonies, and in some respect irrefutable, to any person who accepts the moral imperative as absolute! But must the imperative necessarily be interpreted as "the voice of *God*"? If we mean by that term the God (personal or superpersonal) of monotheist believers, the absoluteness of the imperative appears not necessarily to imply a specifically religious determination of the absolute. I tend to agree with Karl Jaspers's assessment:

> Although in conscience I am confronted with transcendence, I do not hear the transcendent or listen to it as a voice from another world. The voice of conscience is not God's voice. In the voice of conscience the Deity remains silent. . . .[12]

Jaspers's denial may be too categorical. For there is a sense in which obligation undeniably confronts us as divine in origin. To one who already believes, conscience and its inexplicably absolute imperative is likely to be perceived as derived from such a divine source. That was Kant's own position in *Religion Within the Limits of Reason Alone* and that, I strongly suspect, was Newman's true insight—since elsewhere he declares himself incapable of erecting an irrefutable proof of God's existence. Even religious believers who remain skeptical about a direct identification of God with the moral obligation will accept that God sanctions the voice of conscience. This insight undoubtedly adds another dimension, even to a self-discovered morality. But that religious dimension of morality, reserved to the believer, in no way forecloses the possibility of a religiously neutral domain of morality.

A too easy identification of morality with religion may well lead to religiously questionable conclusions, as appears in the now fashionable notion of value. Many well-intentioned believers refer to God as the supreme value, or as the One who preestablishes the values humans ought to pursue. But the modern term value has a highly subjective connotation. It refers primarily to what *we* "value." In thus regarding the human subject as its essential source, we submit God to that subject's projective activity—precisely what Feuerbach declared all religious activity to be. If religion actualizes the person's relation to the absolute, it cannot be a value at all, even though it may *influence* his or her value judgments.

Nor should we consider God to be the One who preestablishes values. To do so, Sartre pointed out, undermines the essential creativity of human freedom. Freedom must do more than ratify preexisting values: it must invent them, imagine them, create them. Freedom can tolerate a great deal of conditioning and restraint. It is always forced to operate within a situation that it has not chosen. But to have its goals and values divinely established would destroy its very essence. God is the *foundation* of value-*creating* activity, not the One who defines values.

A RELIGIOUS INSPIRATION FOR MORAL STRIVING

The conclusions of the preceding discussion have turned out to be somewhat negative. It appears that a common morality requires no religious support for meeting our ordinary obligations, even though, all would agree, a religious inspiration may enhance our motivation for doing so. But to view the matter only in that light presents less than the whole picture. For a fuller vision we ought to change the perspective and ask ourselves the question: What happens when religion becomes the inspiring source of a person's moral endeavor? Does it contribute any significant element that, without its impact, would be missing even in a "common" morality? I shall devote this final section to that question. My answer consists of three parts. First, a religious vision transforms the very notion of what is good. Second, the religiously motivated person continues to invent new values that may later become generally accepted. Third and finally, only religion teaches how to live with moral failure, a failure that marks all human striving.

1. Mature religion creates a particular *ethos*, more comprehensive and open than a closed societal *ethos* can be, even if society attempts to remain above ideological divisions. All morality remains contextual: either its boundaries are defined by principles dominant in a particular society or it transcends the society within which it exists through a more universal but never purely abstract source of inspiration and sanction, such as a religious community. We may easily find examples of both instances. In his remarkable study, *A Theory of Justice* (1972), John Rawls laid down a fundamental principle of social ethics that by its ideological blindness and its mathematically strict norm of equality would impose itself, he hoped, on all unprejudiced parties. Despite his impressive achievement, it did not take critics long to point out that what he was describing as an impartial, humane, and universalizable goal presented in fact the social ideal of the liberal, educated segment of U.S. society. This ideal remains praiseworthy, but it is less than the conclusion of an argument based exclusively on pure reason.

Yet once we have recognized the inevitable conditioning of our moral striving, the question returns: Which context is likely to guarantee the greatest openness of our morality? I would think, with Bergson, that ideally it is the one inspired by the attitude most open to transcendence. I have qualified my answer by the words "ideally" and "open" to avoid identifying its realization with each and every religious normatization of human behavior. We have already conceded that religion may in fact be one of the most divisive factors, even in modern society. We might add that it often violates the elementary principles of a common morality.

Obviously, the rule of religion as a universalizing factor calls for important distinctions. Henri Bergson in *The Two Sources of Morality and Religion* distinguishes a "closed" morality, usually driven by a "closed" religion, from an "open" morality inspired by an "open" religion. A closed morality serves the particular interests of the group by protecting it against those of others, at whatever price. A closed religion hardens this attitude, and secular moralists are right in preferring to such a tribal particularization a religiously neutral, universal respect for elementary human rights. But the morality inspired by an *open* religion raises its ideals not only beyond the group, but also beyond the limits of the values that are more or less universally accepted in modernized societies. In the eyes of such a religiously inspired person, many of these "universal" principles appear inadequate to satisfy the high ideals to which he or she feels called.

The difference in "valuation" dawned on me in a very concrete way some years ago when a woman who had adopted a child was shortly afterwards approached by the same maternity nurse who had been instrumental in the original transaction with a request that she adopt another, still unborn infant. Rather surprised by the request, the woman firmly declined. Three weeks later the nurse contacted her friend again to express her relief that she had not committed herself to the proposed adoption. The infant had been born anencephalic. Its totally undeveloped brain would prevent it from ever sitting up, speaking, or even feeding itself. At that point, the woman said, "In that case, I'll take it." One may interpret her motives for this heroic deed in any number of ways. To me, it clearly meant one thing: to care for a human being that could not care for itself was, from her religious perspective, a *good* thing—not a sacrifice, certainly not an obligation, not even a deliberate act of virtue, but a recognition that caring for helpless life is intrinsically desirable and *therefore* also emotionally satisfactory.

The current vociferous debate over abortion is not likely to result in any kind of lasting agreement, because what one party considers bad, the other holds to be intrinsically good, namely, the preservation of initial human life under highly adverse circumstances. (This religious "openness" is, of course, lacking in some pro-life groups using tribal tactics to enforce their position.) In this dilemma as in some others, secular moralists may regard as foolish or even immoral, in any case not to be imposed as a universal principle, what religiously inspired people consider universally normative. The religious perspective, or absence thereof, fundamentally changes the value coefficient. An open religion extends the range of responsibility by broadening that of value and love.

2. Most important, however, in the development of ethical thought has been the role of the religious imagination. If we have refined our moral sensitivity over the years, that refinement is largely the result of the inventive power of religious women and men who were not even primarily concerned about morality. The concrete realization of moral law requires the imagination to *invent* values that never existed. A purely philosophical study of ethical principles and of their prudential application to individual cases in casuistics is indispensable. But the logic of ethics analyzes, discusses, and applies *existing* rules. Saints invent new rules: they subject to moral responsibility what before was morally neutral territory—neither moral nor immoral. Most denizens of an enlightened society agree that we ought to be kind to others. But does that rule not defeat its purpose when it leads a person to lay down his life for an unknown who may contribute less to society that he or she does, or to devote one's time and energy to the incurable, or to prefer a life of serious hardship to terminating a pregnancy? The remarkable thing about those whom we consider "saints"—those whom the church defines as persons of heroic virtue—is that their outstanding deeds are not demanded by common morality at all. A great deal has been written about the "ethics" of the gospel. Yet what strikes one at first reading is how few concrete *obligations* the gospel introduces and how, instead, it insists on a change of attitude. What we would call "counsels" appear to outweigh strict commandments. "If you want to be perfect, go and sell all you have . . ."They are ideals of a wholly different kind, challenging the person to what surpasses self-achievement—and to what *therefore* must be gratuitous.

Did Francis of Assisi commit a "moral" act when he embraced the leper, or when he gave up his present and future possessions? Gestures such as those, in some respects questionable and in all respects "useless," are in themselves, at best, morally "neutral." Yet Francis transformed them into symbols of a higher moral demand. Must we call Mother Teresa surpassingly "moral," because of what she does for dying paupers? Somehow the term seems strangely inappropriate to describe one so little concerned about established rules. From a utilitarian perspective there appears to be little in favor of the choice of her beneficiaries. If she wanted to augment the general well-being of the human race, is it not a waste of generous energy to pick the dying up from the street, rather than to improve the lot of the living? Clearly, her endeavors move beyond the established into new territory. The amazing achievement of those irresponsible mystical "inventors" is, however, that they, despite an apparent lack of "moral" concern, raise the general moral sensitivity. Others, observing them, are first surprised, then become attracted to follow them. Some of what began as the gratuitous action of a single individual becomes incorporated into our moral *patrimonium* and the exception becomes part of the common ideal. If my analysis is at all right, we cannot but paradoxically conclude that only those not particularly concerned about morality are capable of transforming it. It takes a transcendent vision (which, until now, has almost always been a religious one) to advance moral attitudes beyond the constraints of the past toward a more inclusive future. Writers of textbooks on ethics have rarely raised moral standards, though they have occasionally lowered them.

3. Finally, religion's most significant but least appreciated contribution to moral striving may well consist in assisting us in dealing with failure. Unfortunately all moral endeavor results in some failure. Our high ideals and lofty desires soon yield to "the reality principle" of everydayness. Our goals have not been met and we gradually become convinced that they will probably never be met. Confronting the wall of our moral limitations we cannot escape feeling discouraged by our lack of accomplishment and even more by the inability to learn from our failures.

At this low point, as Kierkegaard pointed out, the ethical enterprise itself grinds to a halt. Morality provides no rules, at least no helpful ones, for coping with its own undoing. Precisely at this moment of failure religion steps in, empowering the individual to salvage his integrity from even the most lamentable defeat. Religion, especially the Christian one, enables me to *accept* my failing self, while at the same time repudiating the moral failure. Where moral reason ceases to justify me, repentance subjects me to a judgment beyond the moral order, at once more demanding and more forgiving.

To the religious person, the moral judgment over his or her conduct is not the ultimate one. Even one willing to die for a moral cause refuses to take ethical rules with *ultimate* seriousness. Such an attitude may appear shocking to the moral humanist for whom the moral judgment is indeed decisive. To the average believer, religion may not bring the higher moral standard, the greater perfection, the ethical innovation, but it may yield what is perhaps even more needed for continuing to live his or her life with dignity, namely, the comforting certainty that sins will be forgiven. Forgiveness may seem a rather dubious contribution to moral striving. It would be, if religion did not work on both sides of the moral scale: inspiring heroism at the top and consolation at the bottom. Both are equally essential, as Chesterton understood: "If a thing is worth doing, it is worth doing poorly."

NOTES

1. Emile Durkheim, *Moral Education* (New York: Free Press of Glencoe, 1961), 6.

2. Alasdair MacIntyre, *After Virtue*, 2d ed. (Notre Dame, Indiana: University of Notre Dame Press, 1984), 38-39. On the "extended" view of morality, see Anthony Cua, "Hsun Tzu's Theory of Argumentation" in *Review of Metaphysics* 36(4): 869-876.

3. Iris Murdoch, *The Sovereignty of Good* (London: Routledge & Kegan Paul, 1970), 92.

4. Epictetus, *Arrian Discourses*, Loeb Classical Library edition, trans. W.A. Oldfather (New York: G.P. Putnam's Sons, 1926), 4.10.

5. W.G. MacLagen, *The Theological Frontier of Ethics* (New York: Macmillan, 1961), 25.

6. Immanuel Kant, *Religion Within the Limits of Reason Alone*, Preface to the First Edition, trans. Theodore M. Greene and Hoyt H. Hudson (LaSalle, Illinois: Open Court, 1934; reissued Harper & Brothers, 1960), 3.

7. Erich Adickes: *Kants Opus Posthumum* (Berlin, 1920), 808.

8. Norman Kemp Smith, *A Commentary to Kant's Critique of Pure Reason*, 2d ed. (London: Macmillan & Company, Inc., 1923), 638.

9. Hans Küng, *Does God Exist?* trans. Edward Quinn (New York: Doubleday, 1980), 578.

10. Edouard Le Roy: "Le problème de Dieu" in *Revue de Metaphysique et de Morale* (1907). Republished in *Le problème de Dieu* (Paris: Cahiers de la Quinzaine, 19:11 [1929]), 202.

11. John Henry Newman, *A Grammar of Assent* (New York: Doubleday-Image, 1955), 101.

12. Karl Jaspers, *Philosophie* II (Berlin: J. Springer, 1932), 272. (My translation.)

5

The Challenge of the Biblical Renewal to Moral Theology

THE PRESENT SITUATION

The Second Vatican Council (1962–1965) was a watershed in the discussion of scripture and moral theology. Yet, here, as in other areas, the originality of Vatican II can be exaggerated. In the decades immediately preceding Vatican II, moral theology was in great flux. As Vincent McNamara notes in his excellent survey of recent Roman Catholic moral theology, "There emerged in Roman Catholicism a strong current of dissatisfaction with the morality of the manual [of moral theology] and an urgent call for a renewal of moral theology."[1] The principal criticisms were directed at the rationalism of moral theology, its lack of emphasis on the distinctive Christian vocation, and its neglect of the bible, especially the New Testament.[2] Catholic moral theology was based almost exclusively on the natural law. Use of the bible was limited mainly to allusions to the decalogue and the command of Jesus to love God with one's whole heart, mind, and soul and the neighbor as oneself (with little attention, however, to the perfection of this command shown by love of enemies, [Matt 5:43-48]). Biblical texts were cited mainly as garnish on a rich stew of arguments concocted from reflection on the natural law and traditional church teaching.

In his magisterial study of the development of moral theology, John Mahoney notes that the stress on auricular confession from the thirteenth-century onward bequeathed to moral theology a threefold and not always helpful legacy: preoccupation with sin, concentration on the individual, and obsession with law.[3]

Immediately prior to the Council, important and influential works such as Gerard Gilleman's *The Primacy of Charity in Moral Theology* and Bernard Häring's *The Law of Christ* called for a moral theology based less on law and more on Christian love and one in conscious dialogue with the biblical teaching.[4] At Vatican II, one of the strongest

calls for the renewal of moral theology came in a speech by Maximos
IV, Patriarch of Antioch, on October 27, 1964, who said: "Current teaching is too marked by a legalism of a past age and entirely imbued with
Roman law. Our Christian moral teaching should have a christocentric
character. It should be an expression of love and liberty."[5]
   The Patriarch went on to criticize the negative quality of moral
theology and its preoccupation with sin and called for the creation of
"a commission of theologians charged to study in light of the Gospel
and the tradition of the Fathers, with openness of heart and sincerity of
faith, moral teaching in general and the commandments of the Church
in particular."[6] Later during the debate on the draft of the document
for priestly formation (November 14, 1964), Paul-Emile Cardinal Legér,
Archbishop of Montreal, seconded Patriarch Maximos's view and
added, "I propose therefore that some section of the schema treat
explicitly of training in moral theology. It is necessary to affirm the
necessity of linking moral theology closely to dogmatic theology, of
basing it on scripture, and of integrating it into the mystery of Christ
and salvation."[7]
   This concern for the renewal of moral theology coincided with
the renewal of biblical studies, which had made slow progress since
the encyclical of Pope Leo XIII on biblical studies, *Providentissimus
Deus* (1893), but which was given new life by the encyclical *Divino
Afflante Spiritu*, issued by Pope Pius XII on September 30, 1943 (the
feast of St. Jerome), to commemorate the 50th anniversary of Leo XIII's
encyclical.[8] Here Pius rejects those Catholic conservatives who "pretend . . . that nothing remains to be added by the Catholic exegete of
our time to what Christianity has produced."[9] The letter also approved
historical-critical methods urging that exegetes "endeavor to deter-
mine the particular character and circumstances of the sacred writer,
the age in which he lived, the sources written or oral to which he had
recourse and the forms of expression he employed."[10]
   Exegesis of the text was to be determined by the literal (or literary) sense defined as "the literal meaning of the words, intended and
expressed by the sacred writer" and while exegetes were also exhorted
to "disclose and expound [the] spiritual significance intended and
ordained by God," they should "scrupulously refrain from proposing
as the genuine meaning of Sacred Scripture other figurative senses."[11]
An important by-product of the biblical renewal fostered by *Divino
Afflante Spiritu* was a realization that biblical revelation was conditioned by its historical circumstances and, therefore, that the moral
teaching of the bible was itself historically conditioned.
   In its *Dogmatic Constitution on Divine Revelation (Dei Verbum)*, Vatican II bestowed the mantle of conciliar authority on the use of histori-

cal criticism, which had maintained a tenuous toehold in the church since the encyclical of Pope Pius XII, *Divino Afflante Spiritu*, in 1943. The Council also called scripture the "soul of theology" and the *Decree On The Training Of Priests* (*Optatum Totius*), states:

> Special attention needs to be given to the development of moral theology. Its scientific exposition should be more thoroughly nourished by scriptural teaching. It should show the nobility of the Christian vocation of the faithful, and their obligation to bring forth fruit in charity for the life of the world.[12]

Today it is difficult to sense the revolutionary impact of such a statement. While the Council may have given marching orders for a revolution, it offered few concrete suggestions on how moral theology was to draw from scripture, or how lay people were to bring scripture to bear on their apostolate in the world.

The initial impact of Vatican II's call for a renewal of moral theology was manifest in a number of studies that called for moral teaching based on biblically informed categories of love (especially the love command in the Gospel of John) and the call to discipleship of all Christians.[13] Vincent McNamara sums up the initial response to Vatican II:

> What we have seen in these first two decades of renewal [that is, the 1950s and 1960s] can be fairly described as a revolution in Roman Catholic theology. It produced an approach to morality that would have been unthinkable for and unrecognisable to the neo-Scholastic. But the result was, not unnaturally, some confusion about method, especially about the justification of moral positions and of moral obligation.[14]

McNamara goes on to note that "clear and well-tried natural law morality had been replaced by something much more woolly."[15]

The initial euphoria about the contribution of scripture to moral theology soon yielded to an often acrimonious inner-Catholic debate mainly among European theologians and biblical scholars that began in the early 1970s and has continued to the present. The debate centers on the somewhat narrow question of whether there is a distinctive and specific Catholic moral theology that is revealed in scripture.[16] On one side stands the "moral autonomy" school, associated with the German moral theologians Alfons Auer, Bruno Schüller, and Josef Fuchs, who are followed in the United States by such well-known moral theologians as Charles Curran and Richard McCormick; on the other side stand the *Glaubensethik* proponents (literally, an ethics of belief or faith), including exegetes Heinz Schürmann and Rudolf Schnackenburg and theologians Hans Urs von Balthasar and Josef Ratzinger.[17] The fundamental question is whether the bible provides any distinctive moral teaching that is not accessible, at least in principle, to human reason (as affirmed by the moral autonomy school) or whether biblical revelation gives a new *content* to morality (the position of the *Glaubensethik* school). Advocates of the moral autonomy school argue that the primary function of scripture is to provide "paraenesis," encouragement or exhortation to do what one already knows as moral.[18]

While it would be beyond the scope of the present treatment to repeat McNamara's excellent journey through this debate, or to attempt any adequate evaluation of it, I will offer a few reflections from the perspective of biblical studies primarily in the United States context.

First, both sides employ a fairly narrow and inadequate understanding of biblical revelation, often identifying it with statements, commands, laws, norms of behavior. Reflection on biblical revelation by exegetes and theologians such as Avery Dulles stress the historical and experiential dimension of revelation that takes place in people's lives and which is expressed in a wide variety of literary genres, narratives, psalms, apocalyptic visions, and parabolic discourses.[19] It seems as if the major guideline for biblical interpretation in *Divino Afflante Spiritu* and *Dei Verbum* have been forgotten, namely, that proper understanding of a biblical text demands attention to the literary genres and customary modes of speaking of the biblical authors.

Second, both sides often seem to work with a fairly narrow view of ethics by focusing primarily on issues of obligation (deontology) while not stressing the contribution of the bible to larger issues of character and disposition. James Gustafson, perhaps the premier moralist in the United States, argues that the scripture offers "revealed reality" rather than "revealed morality."[20] This "revealed reality" provides the foundation for Christian ethics, not simply natural law. The bible's deeper vision of humanity and humanity's relation to God is of importance to Christian ethics, rather than its specific commands.

Third, the debate has been marred by the quest for what is "distinctive of" or "specific to" Christian morality. Much of what has been thought to be "distinctive" to the bible has been found to be present in the ethos of many cultures of the ancient Near East. Perhaps a better word would be "characteristic," which could be used for a biblical perspective that spans many books and many centuries and ultimately represents a perspective which, while not "distinctive," is clearly not found in any other religious tradition in quite the same way as it appears in the bible.[21]

Fourth, for the most part the debate took place in ignorance of the new ecumenical climate following Vatican II. Rarely was the work of European non-Catholic scripture scholars and theologians invoked or consulted, though some of the most significant work in Europe itself was being done by non-Catholics.

Finally, the debate has a particularly European flavor and has for the most part ignored the United States, which has produced some of the most significant biblical exegesis of the post-Vatican II period, and where both moral theology and biblical studies are done in a conscious ecumenical climate.

The present situation in the dialogue between scripture and ethics is at best ambiguous, and the blame cannot be laid at the door of moral theologians. Biblical studies is in danger of evolving into what Edward Farley in his most recent work, *The Fragility of Knowledge: Theological Education in the Church and the University*, has called a "specialty field." Farley contrasts a specialty field to a discipline, which is described as "a paedagogical area that exists in a teaching and learning situation in which the teaching and learning are facilitated by the pursuit of scientific, scholarly inquiry."[22] In contrast, a specialty field is described as "an area of cognitive undertaking which has assumed certain features of professionalization, and which is focused on a sufficiently restricted set of problems to be able to generate published research in a short time."[23] Four historical conditions combine to make a specialty field: (1) the professionalization of the scholar-teacher, (2) the reward system of the modern university, (3) the paradigm of narrowed empiricism, and (4) the ascendancy of the isolated specialty. One of the by-products of the emergence of specialty fields is the rise of "surfeited specialties," where scholars search for a province within the specialty field to make their own, so that "to carve out a special niche, aspiring scholar-specialists must settle for scrutiny of narrower and narrower sets of problems.[24]

I would suggest that contemporary biblical studies is in danger of ceasing to be a discipline within the larger discipline of theology and is becoming rather a collection of "specialty fields." People are becoming authorities and pouring forth streams of articles not on the gospels, or even on a particular gospel, but on recherché methodological studies of a small segment of one of the gospels. A minimal body of textual material often provides the basis of an avalanche of published material. For example, between 1981 and 1989 over twenty-five published books, nearly two hundred articles and (surprisingly) only eight dissertations were published on "Q," a reconstructed document of roughly 225 verses that Matthew and Luke share in common but which are not found in Mark.[25] The medieval allegorists who believed that an inexhaustible treasure of hidden meanings could be found in every biblical verse would recognize contemporary specialists as their intellectual cousins.

The net result, however, is that moral theologians who turn to exegesis often find little help in determining what the bible says on a particular issue. Many biblical scholars have forsaken the challenge of hermeneutics and seem to be settling back into the more comfortable role of social historians or social anthropologists. For example, Bruce Malina, who along with Jerome Neyrey and Jack Elliott is an advocate of the application to the New Testament of the methods of cultural anthropology pioneered by Mary Douglas, argues that the principal contribution of the New Testament to contemporary morality is to show that the people of the first century are different from contemporary people, and thus their ethics and ethos have little contemporary relevance.[26]

Yet, despite overspecialization and the lack of a comprehensive hermeneutical theory, biblical studies have made major contributions to moral theology. Without staking claim to adequacy or comprehensiveness, I would like to highlight seven major contributions.

CONTRIBUTIONS OF BIBLICAL STUDIES TO MORAL THEOLOGY

1. The first major contribution of the New Testament to moral theology is simply informational and descriptive. Virtually every exegete has claimed that New Testament ethics does not exist in a technical sense; the New Testament is not and does not contain a systematic treatise on the principles and practice of Christian life. Rather, exegetes use terms such as "the moral world" or the "ethos" of early Christianity or "New Testament ethics" in a less technical sense to describe early Christian behavior.[27] New Testament scholars also distinguish between biblical or New Testament ethics and "Christian Ethics." While biblical ethics is the source and foundation of "Christian ethics," they are not materially the same.

The writings of the German scholar Rudolf Schnackenburg provide an index of the expansion of New Testament ethics. In 1954 as part of a German series, *Handbuch der Moraltheologie*, he published a short description of New Testament ethics. A revised and expanded edition was published in German in 1962 and translated into English in 1965 as *The Moral Teaching of the New Testament*.[28] This nomenclature quickly became the standard for Catholic moralists who sought to engage the New Testament. In 1986 and 1988, Schnackenburg published a two-volume work by the same title (*Die Sittliche Botschaft Des Neuen Testaments*), which is not simply a revision of the earlier work but a major synthesis of the developments in biblical studies since the Second Vatican Council.[29]

Since biblical studies is the most ecumenical of all the theological areas, Catholic moral theologians and ethicists, especially in the United States, draw profitably on the work of scholars such as Victor Furnish, *Theology and Ethics in Paul*, Wolfgang Schrage, *The Ethics of the New Testament*, and Alan Verhey, *The Great Reversal: Ethics and the New Testament*.[30]

Normally such studies begin with a description of the kingdom proclamation of Jesus and the enactment of this proclamation in his ministry.[31] Jesus is described as part of a larger reform movement within the Judaism of his day and as one who summons people to a renewed sense of the claims of God in human life. His ethics is radically "theocentric." The imminence of God's reign demands a *metanoia*, a change of heart (Mark 1:14-15 and parallels). The dual command to love God with one's whole heart, mind, and soul and to love one's neighbor as oneself is seen as the substance of the ethics of Jesus (Mark 12:28-34 and parallels).[32] Jesus specifies this love in a special way by reaching out to sinners, tax collectors, and others on the margin of society and by forming a community of disciples who are themselves to embody and hand on his message. He teaches in parables, short powerful stories that often surprise and shock their hearers and raise questions about their own lives.[33] People are asked if they are like the older brother who is resentful of the undeserved forgiveness shown to the prodigal son (Luke 15:11-32), or whether, like the rich man of Luke 12:16-22, they place all their hope and trust in acquired wealth, only to have it snatched away in an instant.

After treating Jesus' ethics and its interpretations in the synoptic gospels, surveys center primarily on the "christocentric" ethics of Paul.[34] Almost universally the distinction is made between Paul's indicative statement of what God has done through the death and resurrection of Jesus and the imperative of how Christians should respond to God's action. Allied to this distinction is another between "proclamation" of the Christ event and "paraenesis," or exhortation on how this event is to influence daily life.

In the case of both Jesus and Paul, significant studies have been produced on issues that are of perennial concern to moral theology and church life. The New Testament teaching on divorce provides an example of the fruitful interchange between biblical scholars and moral theologians. Over the last two decades, studies by biblical scholars such as Raymond Collins, Joseph Fitzmyer, and Bruce Vawter on the divorce texts in the gospels (Mark 10:1-12 and parallels; Matt 5:32; Luke 16:18) and in 1 Corinthians 7:8-16 have yielded a number of important insights.[35] First, the studies question whether Jesus was "legislating" in the divorce texts or reacting to lax Jewish divorce practices that often degraded the woman. Jesus invokes the vision of Genesis (especially 1:27 and 2:24) of a union of man and woman in an interdependent and mutually committed relationship. Second, close reading of the texts in their historical and literary context shows that both Paul and Matthew present a definite exception to the teaching of Jesus in view of the pastoral needs of their respective communities. In short, the New Testament offers a double perspective on divorce. The tradition of Jesus mandates that marriage as intended by God be protected; at the same time it offers pastoral accommodations to situations wherein the marriage can no longer be sustained. The contemporary church builds on this legacy by standing in prophetic opposition to a climate of divorce that destroys the love and life that God intended for man and woman. At the same time, through its revised and simplified procedures in marriage tribunals, it continues the "pastoral dimension" of Matthew and Paul.[36]

2. The second major contribution of descriptive New Testament ethics is that paradoxically the New Testament warns against making moral theology the paramount theological enterprise. Especially in the United States, the major religious issues tend to be ethical. The U.S. bishops issued two major and well-publicized documents on ethical issues, the morality of war and a just approach to economic issues.[37] In graduate departments of theology throughout the country, the fastest growing areas are moral theology and ethics. This trend raises some serious problems. It may reflect the heritage of American pragmatism with its penchant toward the concrete and the practical. Even before the theological renewal that followed Vatican II, moral theology was the principal area in which American Catholic theologians were internationally respected. At present, the next generation of moral theologians are being trained in departments in which ethics has become virtually an independent subdiscipline. Given the complexity of ethics itself, many of these programs require virtually no dialogue with biblical studies and theology.

The New Testament counters such tendencies. I will base my arguments on the writings of Paul. Paul's letters are not theological treatises, but occasional pieces, dictated often by pastoral problems with ethical overtones—at Corinth, for example, by rivalry and divisions in the community (1 Cor 1-4), along with such particular problems as a case of incest (1 Cor 5:1-13), lawsuits before pagan judges (1

Cor 6:1-11), "casual fornication" (1 Cor 6:12-20), and the eating of food offered in pagan sacrifices (1 Cor 8-10).[38] These problems occasion the theological reflections that are the foundation of Paul's response to ethical issues. The structure of his letters reflects this development: a more theological first part is followed by a *paranaetic* or hortatory section. A concrete example may help.

Throughout 1 Corinthians, Paul addresses different questions raised by the Corinthians. In Chapter 11, he turns to problems in the liturgical assembly. The first verses are an enigmatic section urging women to wear head coverings when prophesying (1 Cor 11:3-17). The second, longer part of the chapter treats a serious problem surrounding the celebration of the Lord's supper.[39] At Corinth the supper of the Lord was celebrated in the context of an ordinary meal as Christians gathered in the evening at the end of an ordinary working day. The only place with enough space for a community gathering would normally have been the home of one of the more prosperous members of the community.

Paul addresses the problem directly. "I heard that when you meet as a community (as a church), there are divisions among you"; he then gives his initial judgment on the situation: "when you meet in one place, then, it is not to eat the Lord's supper, for in eating, each one goes ahead with his own supper, and one goes hungry, while another gets drunk" (1 Cor 11:20-21).[40]

Thanks principally to the work of Gerd Theissen, we are able to see that this theological quarrel had a social and ethical dimension.[41] Apparently the more prosperous members of the community simply became hungry and tired waiting for the small artisans and day laborers to arrive after a working day that stretched from dawn to dusk. They began the celebration of the Lord's supper with special food and drink that they had prepared for themselves rather than sharing it with others.

Paul reacts strongly to this practice: "Do you not have houses in which you can eat or drink?" (1 Cor 11:22) and highlights the evil effect of this practice: "Do you show contempt for the church of God, and humiliate those who have nothing" (the Greek here is literally, "the have nots"). Paul is saying, in effect, that the social distinctions between upper and lower class people that are part of the fabric of the Hellenistic world have no place in the Christian assembly. One may recall here Paul's early statement to the Galatians that in Christ there is neither Jew nor Greek, slave nor free, male and female (Gal 3:28).

After this initial programmatic assault on the position of those who were shaming the have nots, Paul cites the tradition of the institution of the eucharist, which is parallel to accounts found in the synoptic gospels (1 Cor 11:23-26; Mark 14:22-25 and parallels). Having evoked this tradition, Paul then applies it to the situation in the community. He first says that anyone who eats the bread or drinks the cup of the Lord unworthily will have to answer for the body and blood of the Lord (11:27) and that anyone who eats and drinks without discerning the body eats and drinks judgment on himself (11:28). These statements merit further exploration.

For Paul the words of institution make present again the self-offering of Christ, "my body for you." The "you" are all Christians equally. As Paul has noted in other places, the death of Jesus is an example of one who did not choose his own benefit but that of others, and it shows that Christ died for the weak or marginal Christian brother or sister as well as for the powerful (see also 1 Cor 8:11, "the weak person . . . for whom Christ died," and Rom 15:1-3, the tender scruples of weaker persons). The practices of the Corinthians are a direct affront to the example of Christ. By preferring their own good and by shaming other members of the community of lower social and economic status, they are making a mockery of the eucharist. This view explains Paul's harsh judgment that when they come together they do not eat the Lord's supper. Paul rejects any notion that the eucharist has an automatic effect.

When Paul says that the one who eats without discerning the body eats and drinks judgment on oneself (11:28), the "body" is a reference not to the body of Jesus (as the later concept of sacrilege affirmed) but the community as the body of Christ (which he will discuss in great detail in the following chapter).[42] "Discerning the body" for Paul means assessing the impact of one's actions on the good of the community, especially in regard to its weaker members, and asking how the actions of the community re-present Christ in the world. For Paul, therefore, ethical decisions are consequent on a prior theological vision and religious experience.

As in 1 Corinthians, the proper celebration of the Lord's supper should be a ground of Christian ethics, so Paul's letter to the Romans underscores the ethical dimension of baptism. In Romans 6:4, Paul writes: "We were indeed buried with him through baptism into death, so that, just as Christ was raised from the dead by the glory of the Father, we too might live in the newness of life."[43] Though the reader might expect that, just as Christians die with Jesus, they might rise up with him, for Paul the effect of being conformed to the Christ event is a mode of ethical action, walking in the newness of life (cf. Col 2:12, "you were buried with him in baptism, in which you were also raised with him through faith in the power of God").[44] For Paul, the Christ event and its celebration in baptism and eucharist are the foundation of ethics.[45]

An important consequence of this view is that Paul's concrete ethical directives are not of primary enduring value. Paul gives concrete directives to his communities that would be offensive to contemporary mainstream Catholic moral teaching. For example, Paul exhorts the Corinthians not to engage in legal disputes before non-Christian judges (1 Cor 6:1-11). Slaves are told not to seek their freedom, but to remain in the condition under which they were called (1 Cor 7:21). Christians are to obey secular rulers as representing "the servant of God to inflict wrath in the evildoer"—even when that secular ruler happened to be the emperor Nero (Rom 13:1-7). Paul makes particularly harsh statements on homosexual activity (Rom 1:26-27; 1 Cor 6:9), which from today's perspective are factually inaccurate and lend themselves to contemporary misuse.[46]

Guidance for constructing a contemporary ethics based on the bible is not found in Paul's specific ethical directives, but in the theological affirmations of his letters, in his vision of the Christ event, and in his understanding of communal life in Christ. Paul is a constant voice against the isolation of ethics from theology.

3. The third area in which the study of New Testament ethics has a major impact on contemporary Catholic moral theology is the dissolution of the distinction between a heroic ethics exemplified in the lives of saints or people with a special vocation and a lesser ethics for the ordinary Christians. Such a perspective was a mainstay of pre-Vatican II moral theology. The ordinary Christian was to live with a rather minimalist observance of moral directives and church teaching. Discipleship in imitation of Jesus was often identified with religious life or a special lay vocation.

Though I could approach this question from the understanding of discipleship in the four gospels, I turn again to Paul. One of the treasures of the Pauline corpus is the "Christ hymn" of Philippians 2:6-11.[47] Here Paul appropriates what many scholars feel is a liturgical refrain first heard by the Christian at his or her baptism.[48] The hymn celebrates Jesus who, though in the form of God, did not regard equality with God as something to be exploited (or held on to), but emptied himself, taking on the form of a slave and becoming obedient to death on the cross. What occasions Paul's citation of the hymn?

Though the specific situation that precipitated the letter to the Philippians is debated, one of the reasons for Paul's letter seems somewhat pedestrian to us today: a dispute between Eudoia and Syntyche, two women who were Paul's co-workers in spreading the gospel (4:1-

2), and who may have been leaders in the community at Philippi. There are hints of other, similar problems in the community. In 1:15-17 Paul alludes to others who proclaim Christ from envy or rivalry, or out of selfish ambition. In his normal fashion, Paul spends little time responding to the particular issues but urges his community to "do nothing from selfish ambition or conceit, but in humility regard others as better than yourselves" and "to look not to your own interests but to the interest of others" (Phil 2:4). It is in this context that Paul cites the Christ hymn. Jesus is the paradigm of one who humbles himself and looks not to his own interests but to those of others. This example of Jesus is invoked not to summon people to martyrdom or heroic virtue but to guide their lives in such mundane things as "battles over turf." The death of Christ is a model for Christians in their daily lives.

4. The fourth area in which New Testament ethics has made major contributions to contemporary ethics is the realization of ethical pluralism at the very foundation of Christian faith. Again, by way of illustration rather than absolute proof, I return to the letters of Paul.

One of the most divisive moral issues in Paul's writings (as in other parts of the New Testament) centers around the eating of forbidden foods. It was a pervasive issue at every stage and in every geographical region of emergent Christianity. It is reflected in Paul's conflict with Peter at Antioch (Gal 2:11-14), in Corinth (1 Cor 8-10), and in Rome (Rom 14-15). In the major challenge faced during the early Palestinian missions—when the Gentile Cornelius is accepted into the church (Acts 10:1-34, especially 13-14) and when the question is debated at the "Jerusalem Council" (see especially Acts 15: 19-20)—observance of ritual purity is joined to the question of openness to the Gentiles. The controversy stories of the gospels reflect early debates over this issue, even in the Palestinian environment (especially Mark 7:1-23). At times this debate took the form of whether non-Jewish converts had to observe the dietary prescriptions on unclean and clean foods. At other times it arose over whether Christians could eat meat sold in the marketplace that was left over from pagan sacrifices, or attend social banquets with overtones of pagan worship.[49]

Though these issues may seem esoteric today, New Testament scholars who draw on social anthroplogy underscore the symbolic power of laws associated with eating.[50] A religious group's concern for the food they take into their bodies reflects an equal concern to guard the body of the community from pollution by outside influence. The threat of ritual pollution exercised the same hold on people in the first century as a rigorous sexual ethic exercises on certain people today. The ability of early Christianity to assimilate new groups and the effectiveness of its missionary enterprise hinged on a resolution of problems in this area.

While Paul addressed the issue of eating food offered in pagan sacrifices in 1 Corinthians, in Romans (written ca. A.D. 58, at the end of his sojourn in Corinth), he turns to the issue of eating ritually unclean foods. At Rome some, most likely a particular branch of Jewish Christians, whom Paul calls "the weak" observed the following practices: they eat only vegetables (14:2); they observe particular religious holidays (14:5); some refuse to drink wine (14:21); they are judgmental of others who do not share their practices (14:3). Some of them with scrupulous consciences are harmed by the conduct of the strong who eat foods that they think are unclean. The strong are persuaded that there is nothing unclean in the Lord, reflecting perhaps the saying of Jesus in Mark 7:15 that "there is nothing outside a person that by going in can defile, but the things that come out are what defile" (cf. Mark 7:18-19).

Though Paul counts himself among the strong and shares their theology, he criticizes their attitudes and actions. They engage in contentious arguments with the weak (14:1) and "reject them with contempt" (14:3,10, *exoutheneo*). Their actions put a stumbling block in the way of others (14:13), which causes such harm that they are in danger of destroying the work of God (14:20).

Paul's answer to this moral dilemma is nuanced. He never yields on his fundamental affirmation that the gospel grants freedom from any form of ritualism or legalism. Yet he exhorts his readers to foster understanding and acceptance of those who feel that things such as food taboos, ascetical practices, and ritual observance are important to their standing before God.

Thus Paul allows significant pluralism in one of the most divisive issues in the early church. The "weak" can continue to observe the ritual laws, but they should not impose their practices on others who (in Paul's view) represent the true application of the teaching of Jesus. The strong, however, are to respect the consciousness of the weak and not drive them from the community. Behind this solution to the problem are strong theological affirmations: "The kingdom of God is not a matter of food and drink, but of justice, peace and joy in the holy Spirit" (14:17); "for the sake of food do not destroy the work of God" (14:20); and we who are strong ought to put up with the failings of the weak, "since Christ did not please himself" (15:1-3).

The debates over the degree to which Jewish law should be observed and imposed on Gentile converts provides one of the most dramatic examples of ethical pluralism in the New Testament. Other examples could be adduced, such as the differing views of the relation to Roman rule in Romans 13 and Revelations 13, the different perspectives on divorce in Mark and Matthew and different attitudes toward women in the Pauline and deutero-Pauline letters. For example, Romans 5:12 states that through one person (Adam) sin entered the world and Eve is never mentioned, but the author of 1 Timothy 2:14 writes that "Adam was not deceived, but the woman was deceived and transgressed." Pluralism in both the foundation and practice of Christian life is not a development from the New Testament, but exists at its very origin.

5. The fifth contribution of Paul's ethical teaching to contemporary ethics is the recognition of the need to combine different sources of authority and reflection. Lisa Sowle Cahill of Boston College has synthesized much of current thinking on a proper method for ethics by proposing four complementary reference points for Christian ethics.[51] These are (1) the "foundational texts" or scriptures of the community, (2) the community's tradition of faith and practice, (3) normative accounts of the human derived from philosophy, and (4) descriptive accounts of the human (that is, of what actually is or has been in human society).

Even while granting the cultural distance between Paul and ourselves, I would argue that Paul employs in analogous fashion these four sources of moral reflection. That Paul uses scripture, in his case the Hebrew scriptures, which he undoubtedly studied in detail during his years as a Pharisee, hardly needs documentation. He constantly draws on scripture not only to sound the mystery of the Christ event, but frequently in ethical discussions. For example, when arguing for his apostolic rights to material support in his ministry (1 Cor 9:3-12), he states: "Am I saying this on human authority or does not the law also speak of these things? Is it not written in the law of Moses (citing Deut 25:4), 'You shall not muzzle an ox while it is treading out the grain'?" and argues in rabbinic fashion that this text is the foundation of the right to remuneration (even though Paul himself will not insist on remuneration). When allowing members of the community to eat meat that had previously been sacrificed to idols, Paul not only invokes the principle that there are really no idols, but quotes Psalm 24:1, "the earth and its fullness are the Lord's" to give scriptural warrant to his view (1 Cor 10:25-26).

Traditions of the community also inform Paul's ethical thought. The words of institution cited during the dispute over the Lord's supper and other sayings of Jesus are handed on to Paul from the tradition of the community (for example, 1 Cor 7:10-11). Community customs and practices assume normative force. In 1 Corinthians 11:16, after a series of convoluted arguments on why women should prophesy only with their heads covered, Paul says "If anyone is disposed to be contentious, we recognize no other practice, nor do the churches of God."

Paul's own experience and that of his converts are sources of ethical directives. Throughout 2 Corinthians, he draws on his experience of God's paradoxical power in the midst of weakness to counter his opponents' claims to moral and religious superiority (for example, 2 Cor 1:8-11; 11:30–12:10). In his bitter dispute with opponents in Galatia who were trying to impose observance of the Jewish law on converts, Paul recalls frequently to the Galatians their experience of the spirit and power of God, and how it made them free sons and daughters of God (Gal 3:23-4:7). He then spells out the implications of this freedom for Christian life and argues that it has an ethical dimension. They are called to freedom, Paul writes, but they should not use their freedom "as an opportunity for self-indulgence" (Gal 5:13). Christian freedom involves the cultivation of virtues that manifest life in the spirit (5:16-24) and exhort us to bear one another's burdens (6:2).

Though no one would claim that Paul was well versed in the major philosophical schools of late antiquity, recent studies have uncovered contacts between Paul and popular Hellenistic philosophy. I list two examples. First, Paul employs the diatribe style common in contemporary Stoic and Epicurean philosophy, which consists of an imaginary or fictive dialogue of moral paranesis or exhortation. This style is reflected most vividly in Paul's dialectical conversation with fictive representatives of Judaism in Romans 2 and 3, and in the series of rhetorical questions in 1 Corinthians 15. Second, Paul adopts the philosophical convention of giving ethical advice by a series of *sententiae* or maxims. In his magisterial commentary on Galatians, Hans Dieter Betz argues that in Galatians 6:2-6, Paul adopts and adapts maxims from contemporary philosophy in sayings such as "Bear one another's burdens and so fulfill the law of Christ," "All must test their own work," and "those who are taught the word must share in all good things with their teacher."[52]

Even though Paul never cites by name any known Hellenistic philosopher, he is clearly in debt to the linguistic conventions of their philosophical discourse and to the central motifs and fundamental maxims that are characteristic of their philosophy. The Christian ethicist today faces no less a challenge. Therefore, the New Testament provides not simply material for ethical reflection but also a paradigm or model of the shape of moral theology.

6. A sixth area in which New Testament studies challenge contemporary ethics is the growing realization that in both method and content the dialogue between the bible and Christian ethics must become communal and pastoral. This suggestion is hardly original,

and I am in debt to the recent work of Lisa Sowle Cahill, Richard Hays, and Elizabeth Schüssler Fiorenza. Cahill notes two significant changes in contemporary ethical thought:

> First, the concerns of *ethicists* have moved from trying to assimilate biblical morality to the model of deductive argumentation to an interest in Scripture as foundational to the formation of communities of moral agency. Second, *biblical* scholars have become more explicitly aware of the social repercussions of discipleship as portrayed in the New Testament.[53]

Richard Hays, primarily on the basis of Romans 12:1-12, says that the church as a "counter-cultural community of discipleship" is the "primary addressee of God's imperatives" and argues that in searching the scriptures our primary question must not be "What should I do?" but "What should we do?"[54] Elisabeth Schüssler Fiorenza has argued that while the older doctrinal paradigm of the bible was replaced in the last 150 years by a historical paradigm, the present situation calls for a "pastoral-theological" paradigm. She describes such a paradigm as follows:

> Centers of pastoral-theological interpretation could gather together a scientific community and facilitate the cooperation of biblical scholars, of priests and ministers, and of the active members of the community of faith in studying the Bible. . . . These centers would have to integrate historical-theological scholarship and the contemporary needs and insights of the community of faith in order to say God's word in a new language, so that the Bible will contribute to the salvation of contemporary people.[55]

I would argue therefore that biblical studies—contrary to the tendencies within graduate theological education—theology, ethics, and pastoral practice, must engage in a four way conversation. This conversation will necessarily be ecumenical since by "church" we must always mean the wider community of believers. The recent process followed by the U.S. bishops while drafting the published letters on peace and the economy provides an instance of such cooperation. The drafting committees were composed of bishops entrusted with pastoral leadership and teaching authority working with theologians, biblical scholars, and people trained in philosophy and the social sciences. Hearings were held throughout the country to draw on the experience and wisdom of believers and nonbelievers.

7. Finally, I would like to suggest that reflection on the New Testament shows that ethical issues emerging in a particular historical context and are often in response to definite historical situations. Neither the teaching of Jesus nor the emergence of early Christian literature can be understood apart from its social and political contexts and the challenges these posed.[56] As a similar challenge faces the church today, I would like to suggest that the social arena provides the *fundamental context* for both ethics and biblical studies. The overriding ethical problems in our society are social. The U.S. bishops realized this fact in their 1986 pastoral letter, *Economic Justice for All*, which has, with the passage of time, gained stature as an accurate description of the ills underlying our society. Preeminent in this letter is a concern for the poor and the powerless in modern society.

While recognizing variations resulting from different historical and social contexts, it is clear that concern for the poor and the marginal is a pervasive aspect of biblical literature from its earliest formulations through every stage of its development. The earliest and the most developed legal codes of Israel, the prophetic literature, and the wisdom literature view treatment of the poor as the touchstone of one's proper relationship to God.[57]

The New Testament is heir to this legacy. Jesus pronounces the poor blessed not because of their poverty, but because the kingdom which he proclaimed will undermine the social values and practices that legitimate such poverty.[58] In Matthew's gospel, the public ministry of Jesus concludes with a vision of judgment in which people are condemned because they did not recognize Jesus as present in the hungry, the stranger, and the imprisoned (Matt 25:31-46).[59] The Lukan Jesus begins his public ministry with good news to the poor (Luke 4:16-21) and the gospel echoes with warnings about the danger of wealth.[60] Paul devotes considerable time and energy to organize a collection from the more prosperous communities of Greece for the poorer communities of Judaea.[61] As we noted earlier, he castigates the Corinthians for allowing social and class distinctions to undermine the meaning of the Lord's supper. The Jewish-Christian letter of James summons its readers to be not simply hearers of the word but doers (1:11) and sardonically mocks those who dispense good wishes to the poor while ignoring their plight (2:1-8). The crescendo of apocalyptic visions of the Book of Revelations reaches its peak in a dirge for the Roman Empire, whose merchants gained wealth from her, and who traded in human lives (Rev 18:9-24).

The proper Christian response to pervasive social inequalities is not simply the much needed immediate help manifest among different church groups and volunteer organizations. What is called for is a new theological and anthropological vision informed by the biblical narratives and a realization that the call to heroic discipleship touches the lives of ordinary Christians. There is a need for both a pluralism of concrete actions and a convergence of different methods. Different groups with widely different talents and training must join to form the kinds of communities envisioned by Lisa Sowle Cahill and Elisabeth Schüssler Fiorenza. The cries of the poor should be heard not only in rectories or in departments of theology, but they should also echo through business schools and departments of economics, especially in a Catholic university. The challenge of the New Testament to moral theology today may seem complex, but again it may be as radically simple as Paul's command to the Galatians, "to bear one another's burdens and so fulfill the law of Christ" (Gal 6:2).

NOTES

1. Vincent McNamara, *Faith and Ethics: Recent Roman Catholicism* (Dublin: Gill and MacMillan; Washington, D.C.: Georgetown University Press, 1985), 14.

2. Ibid., 15-16.

3. John Mahoney, *The Making of Moral Theology: A Study of the Roman Catholic Tradition* (Oxford: Clarendon Press, 1987), 1-36, esp. 27-36.

4. Gerard Gilleman, *The Primacy of Charity in Moral Theology*, trans. W.R. Ryan and A. Vachon (London: Burns and Oates, 1959, French orig. 1952); Bernard Häring, *The Law of Christ: Moral Theology for Priests and Laity* 4 vols., trans. E.G. Kaiser (Westminster, Maryland: Newman Press, 1964, German orig. 1959).

5. William K. Leahy and Anthony T. Massimini, eds., *Third Session Council Speeches of Vatican II* (Glen Rock, New Jersey: Paulist Press, 1966), 196.

6. Ibid., 198.

7. Ibid., 310.

8. English trans. in James J. Megivern, ed., *Official Catholic Teachings: Biblical Interpretation* (Wilmington, North Carolina: McGrath Publishing Co, 1978), 316-342. For early reactions see, A. Bea, "Divino *Afflante Spiritu*: De recentissimis Pii PP. XII litteris encyclicis," *Biblica* 24 (1943): 313-322; F. Braun, *Les études bibliques d'apres l'encyclique de S.S. Pie XII "Divino Afflante Spiritu"* (Fribourg: Libraire de l'Universite, 1946); M. Grunthaner, "Divino *Afflante Spiritu*. The New Encyclical on Biblical Studies," *American Ecclesiastical Review* 110 (1944): 330-337; 111 (1944): 43-52, 114-123. Raymond E. Brown has called *Divino Afflante Spiritu* a Magna Carta for biblical progress, in "Church Pronouncements," *New Jerome Biblical Commentary*, ed. R.E. Brown, J.A. Fitzmyer, and R.E. Murphy (Englewood Cliffs, New Jersey: Prentice Hall, 1990), 1167.

9. Megivern, *Biblical Interpretation*, 331.

10. Ibid. On the importance of historical criticism, see Joseph A. Fitzmyer, "Historical Criticism: Its Role in Biblical Interpretation and Church Life,"

Theological Studies 50 (1989): 244-259, and Raymond E. Brown, "The Contribution of Historical Criticism to Ecumenical Church Discussion," in *Biblical Interpretation in Crisis: The Ratzinger Conference on Bible and Church*, ed. Richard J. Neuhaus (Grand Rapids, Michigan: William B. Eerdmans, 1989), 24-49.

11. Megivern, *Biblical Interpretation*, 328-329.

12. No. 16, in Walter M. Abbot, ed., *Documents of Vatican II* (New York: Association Press, 1966), 452.

13. See McNamara, *Faith and Ethics*, 18-38. McNamara lists the important works as Gilleman, *The Primacy of Charity in Moral Theology*; Fritz Tillmann, *Handbuch der katholischen Sittenlehre*, Vol. 3, *Die Katholische Sittenlehre, Die Idee der Nachfolge Christi*; Vol. 4, *Die Verwirklichung der Nachfolge Christi* (Düsseldorf: Patmos Verlag, 1953), and Bernard Häring, *The Law of Christ*. Though much of Tillmann's work was done in the 1930s, his major influence was prior to and immediately after Vatican II.

14. *Faith and Ethics*, 35.

15. Ibid.

16. McNamara (*Faith and Ethics*) provides the best survey of the debate.

17. See C.E. Curran and R.A. McCormick, eds., *Readings in Moral Theology No. 2: The Distinctiveness of Christian Ethics* (Ramsey, New Jersey: Paulist Press, 1980) for a collection of essays representing both positions. Though it is customary to list Josef Fuchs among the proponents of the "moral autonomy" group, his perspective is considerably more nuanced theologically and more open to biblical studies than others in the debate. See Josef Fuchs, "Moral Theology According to Vatican II," in *Human Values and Christian Morality* (Dublin and London: Gill and McMillan, 1970), 1-55, originally published as "*Theologia moralis perficienda; votum Concilii Vatican II*," in *Periodica de re morali, canonica, liturgica* 55 (1966): 499-548; "The Christian Morality of Vatican II," ibid., 56-75; "Christian Morality: Biblical Orientation and Human Evaluation," in *Christian Morality: The Word Becomes Flesh* (Washington, D.C.: Georgetown University Press; Dublin: Gill and McMillan, 1987), 1-18; "Early Christianity in Search of a Christian Morality: 1 Cor 7," ibid., 83-101.

18. See McNamara, *Faith and Ethics*, 77-79.

19. See Avery Dulles, *Models of Revelation* (Garden City, New York: Doubleday and Co., 1983) and William C. Spohn, "Parable and Narrative in Christian Ethics," *Theological Studies* 51 (1990): 101-114.

20. See "The Changing Use of the Bible in Christian Ethics," in Curran and McCormick, eds., *Readings in Moral Theology*, vol. 4, 140-141.

21. See Norbert Lohfink, *Option for the Poor: The Basic Principle of Liberation Theology in Light of the Bible*. The Bailey Lectures, ed. D. Christiansen (Berkeley: Bibal Press, 1986); "Poverty and the Laws of the Ancient Near East and of the Bible," *Theological Studies* 52 (1991): 34-50.

22. Edward Farley, *The Fragility of Knowledge: Theological Education in the Church and the University* (Philadelphia: Fortress Press, 1988), 34; Farley here continues reflection initially proposed in his *Theologia: The Fragmentation and Unity of Theological Education* (Philadelphia: Fortress Press, 1983).

23. Farley, *The Fragility of Knowledge*, 42.

24. Ibid., 39-40.

25. See David M. Scholer, "Q Bibliography 1981-1989," *Society of Biblical Literature: 1989 Seminar Papers*, ed. David Lull (Atlanta: Scholars Press, 1989), 23-38. The flood of works on Q continues unabated since Scholer's bibliography.

 78 JOHN R. DONAHUE, S.J.

26. See J. Neyrey, ed., *The Social World of Luke-Acts: Models for Interpretation* (Peabody, Massachusetts: Hendrickson, 1991), vii: "With the models and perspectives of this book a reader will be well-equipped to read other New Testament texts and classical documents from the ancient Mediterranean society. By sensitizing themselves to another culture and its social structure, careful readers inevitably learn more of their own society by way of contrast" (J. Neyrey); Bruce Malina, 23: "Nevertheless, we can come to understand our strange and alien biblical ancestors in faith. We can learn to appreciate them and learn to live with their witness even as we must find God in our own contemporary experience."

27. See B. Gerhardsson, *The Ethos of the Bible* (Philadelphia: Fortress Press, 1981) and Wayne Meeks, *The Moral World of the First Christians* (Philadelphia: Westminster Press, 1986). For fine overviews of New Testament ethics, see Pheme Perkins, "Ethics, NT," *Anchor Bible Dictionary*, ed. D.N. Freedman (Garden City, New York: Doubleday, 1992) 2, 652-665; W. Schrage, "Ethics in the New Testament," *Interpreters' Dictionary of the Bible, Supplement*, ed. Keith Crim (Nashville: Abingdon Press, 1976), 281-289 (good overview); J.H. Schutz, "Ethos of Early Christianity," ibid., 289-293.

28. Rudolf Schnackenburg, *The Moral Teaching of the New Testament* (New York: Herder and Herder, 1965).

29. Rudolf Schnackenburg, *Die sittliche Botschaft des Neuen Testaments. Band 1: Von Jesus zur Urkirche.* Herders Theologischer Kommentar zum Neuen Testamentum, Supplementband 1 (Freiburg—Basel—Vienna: Herder, 1986); *Band 2: Die urchristlichen Verkündiger* (1988). As the only major study of New Testament ethics by a Roman Catholic, an English translation is a strong *desideratum*.

30. Victor Furnish, *Theology and Ethics in Paul* (Nashville: Abingdon, 1968), *The Moral Teaching of Paul: Selected Issues*, 2d ed. (Nashville: Abingdon, 1985); Wolfgang Schrage, *The Ethics of the New Testament* (Philadelphia: Fortress Press, 1988); Alan Verhey, *The Great Reversal: Ethics and the New Testament* (Grand Rapids, Michigan: William B. Eerdmans, 1984).

31. See also Bruce Chilton and J.I.H. McDonald, *Jesus and the Ethics of the Kingdom* (Grand Rapids, Michigan: William B. Eerdmans, 1987). Chilton is a biblical scholar and McDonald, an ethicist.

32. See Victor P. Furnish, *The Love Command in the New Testament* (Nashville: Abingdon, 1972) and Pheme Perkins, *Love Commands in the New Testament* (Ramsey, New Jersey: Paulist Press, 1982).

33. See John R. Donahue, *The Gospel in Parable: Metaphor, Narrative and Theology in the Synoptic Gospels* (Philadelphia: Fortress Press, 1988), and Bernard Brandon Scott, *Hear Then the Parable: A Commentary on the Parables of Jesus* (Minneapolis: Fortress Press, 1989).

34. See also Victor Furnish, *Theology and Ethics in Paul*, esp. 162-181.

35. R.F. Collins, *Divorce in the New Testament* (Collegeville, Minnesota: The Liturgical Press, Michael Glazier, 1992) (a major, comprehensive study of the pertinent New Testament texts); J.A. Fitzmyer, "The Matthean Divorce Texts and Some New Palestinian Evidence," *Theological Studies* 37 (1976): 197-226; reprinted in *To Advance the Gospel: New Testament Studies* (New York: Crossroad, 1981), 79-111; B. Vawter, "Divorce and the New Testament," *Catholic Biblical Quarterly* 39 (1977): 528-542, reprinted in *The Path of Wisdom: Biblical Investigations* (Wilmington, Delaware: Michael Glazier, 1986), 238-256; "The

Divorce Clauses in Matt 5, 32 and 19,9," *Catholic Biblical Quarterly* 16 (1954): 155-167.

36. John R. Donahue, "Divorce: New Testament Perspectives," *Month* 14 (1981): 113-120.

37. *The Challenge of Peace: God's Promise and Our Response* (May 3, 1983); *Economic Justice for All: Pastoral Letter on Catholic Social Teaching and the U.S. Economy* (Nov. 13, 1986) (Washington, D.C.: United States Catholic Conference).

38. See Jerome Murphy-O'Connor, "1 Corinthians," *New Jerome Biblical Commentary,* 798-815.

39. In the following analysis I draw heavily on Jerome Murphy-O'Connor, "Eucharist and Community in First Corinthians," *Worship* 50 (Sept 1976): 370-385; 51 (Jan 1977): 56-69.

40. Translation is from the *New American Bible: Revised New Testament* (1986). Other translations of 11:20b *(ouch estin kyriakon deipnon phagein,* "it is not easy to eat the Lord's supper) convey an even stronger condemnation by Paul; for example, "it is impossible for you to eat the Lord's supper" *(New English Bible);* "it is not really to eat the Lord's supper" *(New Revised Standard Version).*

41. "Social Integration and Sacramental Activity," in *The Social Setting of Pauline Christianity* (Philadelphia: Fortress Press, 1982), 145-174.

42. See Murphy-O'Connor, "Eucharist and Community in 1 Corinthians."

43. Translation is from the *New American Bible, Revised New Testament* (1986).

44. See Robert Tannehill, *Dying and Rising With Christ* (Berlin: Alfred Topelmann, 1967).

45. On the christological and sacramental foundations of ethics see Schrage, *The Ethics of the New Testament,* 172-177.

46. The most balanced and scholarly treatment of these difficult texts is Victor P. Furnish, *The Moral Teaching of Paul: Selected Issues,* rev. ed. (Nashville: Abingdon Press, 1985).

47. A full review of the study of this hymn is offered in Ralph Martin, *Carmen Christi: Philippians ii, 5-11 in Recent Interpretation and in the Setting of Early Christian Worship,* rev. ed. (Grand Rapids, Michigan: William B. Eerdmans, 1983).

48. As proposed by E. Käsemann, "A Critical Analysis of Philippians 2:5-11," in *God and Christ,* Journal for Theology and Church, no. 5, ed. R. Funk (New York: Harper Torchbook, 1968), 45-88.

49. Such are the different situations addressed in 1 Corinthians 8-10. See J. Murphy-O'Connor, "Freedom or the Ghetto," *Revue Biblique* 85 (1978): 543-574, and Wendel L. Willis, *Idol Meat in Corinth: The Pauline Argument in 1 Corinthians 8 and 10,* Society of Biblical Literature Dissertation Series, no. 68 (Chico, California: Scholars Press, 1985).

50. Mary Douglas, *Purity and Danger: An Analysis of the Concepts of Pollution and Taboo* (London: Routledge and Kegan Paul, 1966); *Implicit Meanings: Essays in Anthropology* (London: Routledge and Kegan Paul, 1975); Bruce Malina, *The New Testament World: Insights from Cultural Anthroplogy* (Atlanta: John Knox Press,1981); *Christian Origins and Cultural Anthropology* (Ibid., 1986); Jerome Neyrey, "The Idea of Purity in Mark," in *Social-Scientific Criticism of the New Testament and Its Social World,* ed. J. Elliott *Semeia* 35 (1986): 91-128.

51. Lisa Sowle Cahill, *Foundations for a Christian Ethics of Sexuality* (Philadelphia: Fortress Press; Ramsey, New Jersey: Paulist Press, 1985), esp. 1-13. Cahill comments that people responding to her proposal noted that this is a development of the Methodist "quadrilateral" approach to ethics.

52. H.D. Betz, *Galatians*, Hermeneia (Philadelphia: Fortress Press, 1979), 301-307.

53. Lisa Sowle Cahill, "The New Testament and Ethics: Communities of Social Change," *Interpretation* 44 (1990): 384.

54. Richard B. Hays, "Scripture-Shaped Community: The Problem of Method in New Testament Ethics," *Interpretation* 44(1): 47.

55. Elizabeth Schüssler Fiorenza, *Bread Not Stone: The Challenge of Feminist Biblical Interpretation* (Boston: Beacon Press, 1984), 42.

56. Within the last decade there has been renewed interest in the historical Jesus. Recently this development has been referred to as "the third quest" for the historical Jesus in contrast to the original nineteenth-century quest and the "new quest" associated with the disciples of Rudolf Bultmann in the 1950s and 1960s. Some representative works are Marcus Borg, *Jesus: A New Vision* (San Francisco: Harper and Row, 1987); James Charlesworth, *Jesus Within Judaism: New Light from Exciting Archeological Discoveries*, Anchor Bible Reference Library (New York: Doubleday, 1988); *Jesus' Jewishness: Exploring the Place of Jesus in Early Judaism*, ed. James Charlesworth (Philadelphia: American Interfaith Institute; New York: Crossroad, 1991); J. Dominic Crossan, *The Historical Jesus: The Life of a Mediterranean Jewish Peasant* (San Francisco: Harper Collins, 1991), an interesting study of the background and social context of Jesus' ministry, but problematic reconstruction of the life and teaching of Jesus; John P. Meier, *A Marginal Jew: Rethinking the Historical Jesus* (New York: Doubleday, 1991), first of a projected three-volume work; John Riches, *Jesus and the Transformation of Judaism* (New York: The Seabury Press, 1982), and E.P. Sanders, *Jesus and Judaism* (Philadelphia: Fortress Press, 1985).

57. See the studies of Norbert Lohfink and, for the early centuries of our era, the excellent study by Gildas Hamel, *Poverty and Charity in Roman Palestine, First Three Centuries C.E.* (Berkeley: University of California Press, 1990).

58. See J. Dupont, "The Poor and Poverty in the Gospels and Acts," *Gospel Poverty*, ed. M. Guinan (Chicago: Franciscan Herald, 1977), 25-52.

59. The interpretation offered here is somewhat disputed; see J.R. Donahue, "The 'Parable' of the Sheep and the Goats: A Challenge to Christian Ethics," *Theological Studies* 47 (1986): 3-31.

60. See J.R. Donahue, "Two Decades of Research on the Rich and Poor in Luke-Acts," in *Justice and the Holy: Essays in Honor of Walter Harrelson*, ed. D.A. Knight and P.J. Paris (Atlanta: Scholars Press, 1989), 129-144 and John Gillman, *Possessions and the Life of Faith: A Reading of Luke-Acts*, Zacchaeus Studies: New Testament (Collegeville, Minnesota: The Liturgical Press, 1991).

61. See Jouette Bassler, *God and Mammon: Asking for Money in the New Testament* (Nashville: Abingdon Press, 1991) and Dieter Georgi, *Remembering the Poor: The History of Paul's Collection for Jerusalem* (Nashville: Abingdon Press, 1991).

6

Conscience, Discernment, and Prophecy in Moral Decision Making

How we approach our moral decision making has been a matter of continual interest in the Catholic moral tradition through the centuries and remains today a subject of considerable urgency, and not infrequently of controversy. The favored way in which the tradition has historically approached the subject of moral decision making has been in the language of the individual's moral conscience, a theme appropriated by early Christian writers from Greek thought and developed with considerable subtlety and sophistication, as I hope to show in the first part of this essay.

If the ethical tradition of conscience has formed the mainstream of Christian thought through time, it has not, however, been the only current of Catholic reflection concerned with the process of moral decision making. Also running through the ages, in a neighboring valley as it were, is the quiet stream of spiritual reflection, with its more placid religious tradition of discernment as a means of identifying the influence of God and the delicate work of the Spirit in the souls of individuals. And one feature of some recent thinking on Christian moral decision making, influenced partly by the Catholic controversy of the 1950s on situation ethics, has been to accept into the sometimes turbulent waters of ethical thought this more spiritual tradition as a kind of tributary with its own history of experience and analysis and with its own special contribution to offer to contemporary Christians as they face the often anxious choices with which modern society and increased technology confront them.

Moreover, to continue our metaphor, we have in recent times in the Roman Catholic church also witnessed the emergence of a powerful stream that has been running silently underground for centuries: the theological tradition of prophecy. And if it is the case that the spiritual tradition of discernment has fed into the strong ethical mainstream of conscience, then it also appears that the best and most

promising future for the study of Christian moral decision making
consists in recognizing that the tradition of conscience enriched by discernment is itself a tributary that finds its full rationale and Christian
self-identity as it joins the powerful, reemergent theological current of
prophecy in the church and in society.

In other words, what I wish to suggest, and propose to explore, is
the thesis that what has been for centuries an ethical tradition of conscience is strengthened by the accession of the religious tradition of
discernment and finds in turn its fulfillment in the theological tradition
of prophecy. Let us begin with the ethical tradition of conscience.

THE ETHICAL TRADITION OF CONSCIENCE

When the apostle Paul went up to Jerusalem and was arrested and
interrogated by the chief priests and the Jewish Council, he began his
defense by claiming, "Brethren, I have lived before God in all good
conscience up to this day" (Acts 23:1). That statement sums up one of
the major themes of his writings to Christian converts in Corinth and
elsewhere, that of the moral conscience, a term that originated in Greek
philosophy to refer to the experience of self-awareness in the forming
of one's moral judgments. Given the popularity of the theme in Paul,
who uses the term on more than twenty occasions, it is not surprising
that it was taken up and explored by subsequent Christian thinkers as
an inner source of moral evaluation and guidance. Sometimes it is
described metaphorically in terms of God's law written in our hearts,
sometimes as the voice of God addressing us internally, as God gave
moral instructions to the first humans, and sometimes it is represented
as a spark or glimmer of moral enlightenment that still exists in all
humans amid the dark effects upon them of the moral lapse of the first
human couple.

This last interpretation was the teaching of the great fifth-century
linguist and testy misogynist, St. Jerome, who complicated matters for
subsequent theologians by using the rare Greek word *synderesis* to refer
to conscience, whereas Paul and others had used the more common
term *syneidesis*. When theology became a systematic intellectual discipline in the Middle Ages, the scholars of the day attempted to do justice to both Paul and Jerome by understanding Jerome's term of
synteresis as referring to conscience as the innate capacity for moral
reflection that exists in all of us, while using Paul's term *syneidesis* to
refer to the actual exercise or final judgment of our conscience.[1]

Thus, in the majestic Gothic cathedral of theology known as the
Summa Theologiae of the Dominican friar, Thomas of Aquino, we are all
described as possessing a habitual grasp of the basic principles of

morality, or *synderesis*. These moral fundamentals are always there at the back of our minds, as it were, and when we approach moral decision-making, they are brought into the forefront of our thinking to be applied as *syneidesis* in forming moral judgments about the rightness or wrongness of our behavior.

In this interpretation of moral decision making, conscience is no more and no less than an ordinary act of human reasoning applying the various principles of morality to individual situations. For Aquinas and the subsequent Catholic moral tradition up to the present, conscience is not the origin of moral principles, creating morality afresh in every decision. It is the human medium, or created image, of God's own reasoning, or of God's eternal law as the supreme rule of human behavior. It is this role as reflector of God's law that gives conscience its binding force for the individual, and also provides the basis for the respect that others should accord to the individual's conscience, even if it may be genuinely mistaken. As Aquinas explained, no one is bound by any precept except through the medium of his or her knowledge of the precept; and since conscience is the application of knowledge to an action, then conscience is said to bind by force of the divine precept. Moreover, he continues, "when a reason which is in error proposes something as a command of God, to dismiss the dictate of reason is just the same as dismissing the command of God."[2]

It is important to note, however, that though for Aquinas one is always obliged to follow one's conscience even when it is mistaken, such behavior is not always automatically good. Its goodness, or lack thereof, depends on why the mistake arises in the first place and whether we are responsible for it; that is, in the traditional phrase, whether our mistake arises from ignorance that we could, and should, have taken steps to correct.

In the centuries that followed Aquinas, two aspects of conscience occupied moral theologians and the church in general. One was this question of ignorance and the degree to which, if one acted conscientiously but was genuinely mistaken, one could be considered not guilty of sinning even in doing something that is objectively wrong. In this debate, the key phrase is "invincible ignorance," that is, ignorance that cannot be corrected, for whatever reason. As Pope Pius XI expressed it on the eve of the First Vatican Council, in writing of Christians who were not Catholics, "those who are in ignorance of the true religion, if it is invincible, are not guilty of this in the eyes of God."[3] Moreover, as the Second Vatican Council was to express it, "Conscience frequently errs from invincible ignorance without thereby losing its dignity, although the same cannot be said of a person who takes little trouble to find out what is true and good, or when conscience is by degrees almost blinded through a habit of sin."[4] In this way the church was able to take realistic account of the fact that some Christians did not accept the church's claims to their full allegiance, by attributing their falling short of Catholicism to a mind-set and a culture that made it very difficult, if not impossible, for them to acknowledge and shake off their ignorance. It has only been in recent years and in the more ecumenical climate of and since the Second Vatican Council that the church has come to a more positive interpretation of Christian differences, and acknowledged that such Christians share in some measure in the saving truth of Christianity, even if they do not share its Catholic fullness.

The other aspect of conscience that preoccupied moral theology as it developed after the Middle Ages and the Reformation was the question, not of the mistaken conscience, but of the doubtful conscience. If one was in doubt and faced with a dilemma about what one should do, how was one to resolve the dilemma? To answer this basic question of the doubtful conscience, various theories were developed by moral theologians in the sixteenth to the eighteenth centuries; theories that can be summed up in nontechnical language as a choice between, on the one side, looking for authoritative teaching and following it as the safer line of conduct, or on the other side, weighing up the various arguments and choosing to follow the view that seems the more reasonable by comparison with others, or even following any view that appears reasonable and for which a good case can be made. It was this last school, known as probabilism, or the legitimacy in cases of doubt of following a view for which one has some good reason, which gave moral theology and especially the Jesuits a bad reputation for moral permissiveness. This charge came particularly from their mortal enemies the Jansenists led by their most famous exponent, Blaise Pascal, who espoused a much more rigorous and authoritarian approach to morality and matters of conscience, including matters about which the individual's conscience was in doubt.

However, the moral system of probabilism, or of aiming to resolve dilemmas of conscience by rational analysis and the appeal to various authorities, eventually received general acceptance in the church, at least for questions in which no clear church teaching was at stake. It was appealed to by many, for instance, during the fevered debate on contraception in the mid-1960s, when it seemed to many that the church's historical opposition to artificial birth control might be on the point of change. And it is in that historical and technical context that we can best understand the comment by a Vatican press officer in presenting the papal encyclical *Humanae vitae*, which claimed to dispel all doubt on the matter, that although a careful reading of the encyclical did not suggest that it was infallible teaching, nevertheless it was "binding on the conscience of everyone, without ambiguity, and excludes the possibility of adopting a 'probable opinion' in opposition to its teaching."[5]

Of interest to our general theme of conscience in moral decision making is the fact that Pope Paul's encyclical itself addressed the question of conscience and repeated the traditional Catholic position that a correct conscience is the true interpreter of the objective moral order instituted by God.[6] The Pope said nothing, however, about mistaken consciences or about problems arising from ignorance or from doubt, for he also maintained that the interpretation of the natural moral law is the role of the church's magisterium.[7] He implied at least that there could be no room for doubt or ignorance, and certainly not for invincible ignorance, in cases where the magisterium delivered clear teaching on a particular matter, leaving it beyond dispute, as he claimed to be doing in his encyclical.

One effect of that encyclical on contraception was to put various groups and bodies on a collision course from which the Catholic church is still suffering and to introduce an atmosphere of rancor and adversarialism that has spread from the deep divisions on contraception to other areas of moral behavior, to the distress of anyone who is committed to Christ's church on earth, and more than amply fulfilling the statement of the bishops at the Second Vatican Council that the pilgrim church will find itself afflicted by pains and difficulties that come from inside itself as well as those that come from outside.[8] It is, in fact, one of the weaknesses of our Catholic tradition of conscience, as it has developed and is popularly misunderstood, that it tends to be seen in terms of a power struggle, with the claim on one side for respectful obedience to the church's authority as exercised by the pope and bishops in the church, countered on the other side by the claim for the authority of conscience as a court of appeal, and for the right and the freedom to follow one's conscience. What then tends to be obscured in the din and the heat of battle is that the real point at issue is not ethical autonomy or heteronomy, freedom or obedience, but the individual's moral responsibility for her or his own behavior and how this can best be identified and authenticated as God's will. There is a personal uniqueness and a human solitariness about the exercise of moral conscience that is brought out by the Council's statement that there we are alone with God whose voice echoes in our depths. This conscientious communion with God is further expressed in the idea quoted from Pope Pius XII and from Greek thought of conscience as a religious sanctuary.[9] It should be noted, however, that this religious theme does not have implications only for the respect that is owed to the individual's conscience by outsiders. For if conscience is holy ground in the individual on which others trespass at their peril, it is because conscience is the meeting place where one stands naked before God. And this surely has profound implications for the serious personal responsibility to be discharged by the individual in his or her moral decision making.

THE RELIGIOUS TRADITION OF DISCERNMENT

So far we have been considering the subject of moral decision making within the classical tradition of conscience as it was adopted from contemporary ethical thought by St. Paul, who had, in the phrase of C.H. Dodd, a hospitable mind, and as it was developed through the early church and the medieval scholastics into the mainstream of Christian moral reasoning. There it still occupies an important central position, not least in its capacity to offer a common ground and shared terminology for discourse and ethical discussion between Christians and others in society; as well as providing a basis for the claim to a universal human right to freedom of conscience in society, and thus to the personal space to decide and act responsibly in accordance with one's innermost moral convictions.

It is possible, however, to view moral decision making not simply in an ethical framework of reflection on what I ought to do, but in a more formally religious context of what God wishes me to do, or what God is calling or inviting me to do. And within this way of construing moral decision making, moral theology can call into service another current of thought that has developed within the Catholic spiritual tradition and which perhaps indicates a difference of focus between two phrases that are normally considered practically synonymous, "Christian ethics" and "moral theology." The former term of Christian ethics is a product of the Enlightenment, which views morality as the human enterprise of exploring and identifying how humans ought to behave in their dealings with each other. Within that context of ethics one can then inquire what contribution Christianity can make to the human ethical quest. One fruitful result of this proceeding is that Christians find themselves engaged with others in society in the search for common and shared ethical values and for joint approaches to the major ethical issues of the day. But viewing Christian approaches to morality as a species or subset of ethics in general can also raise difficulties. Perhaps the most obvious is the attempt or, for some people, the challenge to identify what specific contribution Christianity has to offer to the shared debate, and whether there are unique features about Christian ethics, as compared with Jewish or Muslim ethics or with secular humanist ethics. If there are such unique Christian contributions then the further problems arise of whether they would make a difference to the solution of contemporary issues, and whether the contribution which Christianity finds itself offering is a truncated or impoverished one, because of the impossibility of communicating and sharing with others the full richness of the Christian interpretation of reality and of moral behavior.

By contrast with the phrase "Christian ethics," the term "moral theology," which first became current in the sixteenth century, implies that inquiry into the moral enterprise is not so much a branch of ethics as a branch of theology. As theology, its primary object is not how humans should behave toward each other, but how God behaves in dealing with us. As moral theology, it is concerned with God's designs and initiatives concerning human creatures and God's continual invitation to them to respond to those initiatives. Viewing the subject of moral decision making within the context of moral theology entails the question of how moral theology relates to other branches of theology. Until comparatively late in this century, moral theology as it had developed had no formal connections with other areas of theological reflection. In more recent times, however, the renewal of moral theology, which was demanded by the church's bishops in the Second Vatican Council, and the requirement of a "better integration of philosophy and theology" has resulted in its attempt to become more formally theological than simply philosophical, as hitherto. And one way in which this has taken place has been in its attempting to draw upon the rich current of spiritual theology within Catholicism, a tradition that was viewed in the past as addressed only to those Christians who aspire to a deep spiritual union with God in the consecrated life, but whose riches have increasingly become accessible to all who aspire to live their baptismal Christian vocation in whichever walk of life they find themselves.

Writing of the changes that had been taking place within the Catholic church in Europe in the middle of this century, in an atmosphere sensitive to existentialism and personalism, Aubert described how conscience had come to be seen as "no longer applying a general principle to a particular case by an automatic syllogism, but more as a faculty which under the guidance of the Spirit of God is endowed with a certain power of intuition and discovery which allows it to find the original solution appropriate to each case."[10] In thus describing a shift from a sometimes excessively rational approach to moral decision making, Aubert was correct so far as he went, but he did not go far enough. In particular, he could have observed that conscience as a power of intuition and discovery was concerned not simply in finding solutions to moral decision making, but in discovering where the Spirit was leading individuals in response to the call of God within the context of their overall vocation to follow the will of God. In this way more justice can be done to the instruction of the Council that moral theology should show the nobility of the Christian vocation of the faithful.

One important way forward for moral theology, then, is to explore how Christian teaching, or *didache*, emerges from within the Christian proclamation, or *kerygma*. We can see this at work in the moral teaching of Jesus in the Sermon on the Mount (Matt 5–7), which was perhaps an early Christian catechism, and which sketches the pattern of life for disciples as they enter into the kingdom which Jesus has just announced and promulgated as the definitive presence of God in this world. It is a pattern of spiritual response to divine invitations that we also find in the great hinge passage of Romans 12 in which Paul describes how Christians should respond in their decision making to the gospel of Christ. As the New English Bible translation expresses it: "Therefore, my brothers, I implore you by God's mercy to offer your very selves to him: . . . Adapt yourselves no longer to the pattern of this present world, but let your minds be remade and your whole nature thus transformed. Then you will be able to discern the will of God, and to know what is good, acceptable, and perfect" (Rom 12:1-2).

To know what is good, acceptable, and perfect, not by consulting one's conscience, but by discerning the will of God: such has been a major purpose of the whole Christian and Catholic current of spiritual theology, and its developing tradition of spiritual discernment. Its basis, of course, is the belief that God communicates with each of us individually in our heart of hearts through the Holy Spirit who is, in John Macquarrie's limpid phrase, "God in his nearness to us." But since we are human, limited, and fallible in our perception of God's touch in our souls, and since we can unconsciously distort or misread the signals through poor reception, that tradition has also been at pains to develop criteria of discernment as a context within which we may find assurance that it really is God who speaks, and that we have the truth of God's self-communication to our inmost selves. For history is littered with the tragedies of people wrongly convinced that God has communicated with them and has bidden them to act thus and thus.

The Roman poet-cosmologist Lucretius had more than ample evidence for his comment on the evil deeds to which religion could lead.[11] But let one example from the Hebrew Scriptures suffice for all the tragic consequences of what Ronald Knox called false religious enthusiasm.[12] The Book of Judges tells us that "the Spirit of the Lord came upon Jephthah" and he vowed that if God gave him victory over the Ammonites he would sacrifice to God the first figure he met at his homecoming—which turned out to be his only daughter rushing out to congratulate him, whom he duly burned to death in thanksgiving (Judg 11:29-39). The comment of Aquinas on the episode is interesting. The prompting to make a vow of gratitude may well have come from God, as Scripture implies, but the actual form that the vow took came not from the Spirit but from Jephthah's lack of discernment. The verdict of Jerome which Thomas records was more trenchant: "Jephthah was a fool to make his vow, and a knave to keep it."[13]

So the question is a real one: how can one tell which moral promptings originate in God and which are the product of our own feelings, prejudices, or states of mind? In its attempt to answer this question, the Catholic tradition of spiritual theology has identified community and personal criteria. The community criteria are based on the belief that God will not be self-contradictory or set at nought the whole enterprise of creation and salvation for any creature. Thus it is to be expected that God's intimations to individuals will not be at variance with the word of God as articulated for us in the bible. It is notorious, however, that the bible can be as much a source of controversy as of enlightenment. The French Reformation leader John Calvin complained that contemporaries twisted the bible to their own purposes as one can the wax nose of a puppet.

And so a further criterion points to the Christian community from which the New Testament emerged and within which it is best understood in each generation and applied to changing circumstances. It is not only that the church is the safest interpreter of scripture; the upbuilding and well-being of the church and of its mission in society are also a major purpose of the New Testament and so form a controlling factor in how it is to be understood and applied. St. Paul put it well when he contrasted Christian love as characteristically outward-looking and building up the community, as compared with knowledge that can too easily become a puffing up and self-centered exercise of pride leading to the ultimate destruction of the individual and others in the community (1 Cor 8).

Another way of expressing this ecclesial criterion and one that has come into increasing prominence in recent years, is the idea of *koinonia*, or fellowship, which is characteristically the gift and the goal of Christ's Spirit for the church. Consequently, it can be concluded, anything that is disruptive of the spirit of unity and harmony among Christ's disciples cannot proceed from his Spirit.

Such are the two community criteria of divine consistency and Christian concord, which the Catholic spiritual tradition has developed in scrutinizing moral decision making as the human response to God's intimate call to the individual. Together with their undoubted strength and appeal, however, it is evident that such testing questions put to individual experience are themselves open to some questioning, and increasingly so today. The aim of preserving concord, for example, can be understood either literally as being one in heart, or it can be understood in an extended sense as being in harmony. It does not follow, however, that people who are one in heart are thereby committed to expressing that interior unity in exactly identical ways, for that would, as the truism expresses it, confuse the idea of unity with that of uniformity.

Wives and husbands, for example, who it may be hoped are one in heart may well come to identify with each other and even to take on some of the characteristics of each other, but it does not follow that they should become identical; on the contrary, their oneness of heart should strengthen them in their diversity and mutual harmony. Likewise, the extended idea of concord as harmony is worlds apart from monotonal identity or faultless repetition, as the rich but unified diversity of polyphony is worlds apart from the strong single melody of plain chant. Diversity cannot so easily be discounted, as Karl Rahner pointed out in his study of *The Dynamic Element in the Church*:

> . . . when in the Church's case various influences flow from God into the Church, some through the ministry, others directly to members of the Church who hold no office, it is clear that God alone can fully perceive the meaning, direction and divinely-willed purpose of these. . . . A number of forces like this within the Church here on earth must be felt by human beings themselves as disparate and opposed, precisely because they are unified by God alone. Of course, it is true, as Paul says, that the various gifts of the one Spirit must work together harmoniously in the unity of the one Body of Christ. But since the gifts are one in the one Spirit but do not form one gift, that unity of the Body of Christ itself is only fully one in the one Spirit.[14]

The deeper question raised by these community criteria of divine consistency and Christian concord, and by Rahner's comment on them, relates to the very idea of the church and our understanding of it, both in its history and its extension.

The great Dominican scholar, Yves Congar, observed that in this century we have come increasingly to appreciate the close connection that exists between pneumatology and ecclesiology, the study of God's Spirit and the study of Christ's church.[15] So far as concerns our understanding of the church's activity in the course of time, John Henry Newman once remarked that great acts take time. And just as it is a feature of the church not to be the originator or the initiator of the works of the Spirit in the hearts of men and women but only the authenticator, so that process of recognition and the appropriation of new insights can on occasion be a lengthy one, leading perhaps to the conclusion that it is easier for the church to acknowledge, looking back, that "the finger of God was there, or has been there" than for it to judge in the present that "the finger of God is here." If this be the case, then this criterion of concord cannot be applied in the "meantime," in the interim period during which the Spirit may indeed be at work even if not yet fully recognized.

Further, the traditional criterion of preserving the fellowship, or *koinonia*, of the church has raised questions that affect the church's self-identity, as the recovery of the biblical idea of *koinonia* has become the recognized key to promoting ecumenism, and to stimulating various Christian churches and ecclesial bodies to discover and strive toward the fullness of unity that Christ prayed for among his disciples and which has been so sadly lacking in the past. The Catholic church's *volte-face* in its understanding of the role of the church in the salvation of individuals who are not its members resulted in the Second Vatican Council's recognition that the Spirit of Christ and Christian baptism is operative with sanctifying power among other Christians, with possible consequences for the Catholic church's own upbuilding and its own fuller realization of the mystery of Christ and the church.[16] The possibility cannot be discounted that other Christian bodies can have distinctive contributions and insights to offer concerning community spiritual discernment and moral decision-making, difficult though this may be for some Catholics to accept.

It appears evident, then, that the community criteria that have traditionally been called on to help discern the possible influence of the Spirit in the hearts and minds of individuals are difficult to apply in any conclusive manner; and it is here that other more personal criteria can come into play as these have developed in the tradition of spiritual theology. Indeed, it may well be that precisely because of the contemporary difficulties that affect the application of community criteria, those more personal criteria become all the more important.

One feature of the spiritual tradition of personal criteria realizes that a projected course of action that is good in principle and in accordance with biblical or church teaching may not necessarily be God's will for the individual who is considering it. Prayer can result in neglect of duties; asceticism can undermine health; contributions to worthy causes can impoverish one's dependents. All these traditional Christian practices, prayer, fasting, and almsgiving, are obviously good, yet in individual cases they need to be thought through carefully to their probable consequences and in the light of the individual's resources and past experience.

Again, the tradition of spiritual psychology suggests the need to distinguish clearly between, on the one hand, an emotional feeling of loving worship and an intense wish to serve God as experiences that can reasonably be considered to come from God, and on the other hand, a specific impulse for decision or action arising from these experiences that may actually be more of a human "afterglow" of such experiences than an integral part of them. Remember Jephthah!

What these and other personal criteria bring into prominence is the indispensable importance of self-knowledge in the spiritual tradition of discernment. As a wise Jesuit spiritual director, John McMahon, once observed to me, this includes getting to know the order of one's disorders. And this means striving to be aware of one's own motives, character, temperament, and desires as the personal and unique matrix into which we each receive the influx of the Holy Spirit. Not that such personal endowments and characteristics need to be regarded always in a negative manner or as distorting the message. What the tradition does stress, however, is the need to be aware of any capacity for rationalizing or self-delusion that we may possess, and of being as sensitive to our weaknesses as we may be to our strengths.

This need for self-knowledge in turn points to another personal criterion, that of self-control. It is a constant feature of the spiritual tradition, stemming from St. Paul (1 Cor 14:27-34), that gifts of the Spirit can and should be within the reasonable control of the individual. Within the context of the ethical mode of conscience, it is worth recalling the observation of Martin D'Arcy, S.J., in his significantly entitled work, *Facing the Truth*: it is perfectly possible that "when persons refer to conscience they mean an opinion so hotted up that it becomes incandescent; what S.T. Coleridge calls 'phlogiston in the heart.'"[17] For, of course, it is possible to "canonize" one's temperament in the service of the Lord, thus confusing zeal for the truth with a personal penchant for belligerence, or disguising personal timidity in the garb of pastoral prudence. Within the religious and spiritual tradition, Karl Rahner insists on the need for "a defense against facile mysticism and sentimental enthusiasm [which seeks] to avoid the trouble of objective and cautious reflection."[18]

Ultimately these personal criteria come down to the same canons of consistency and concord that I have already considered in a community context, but now they refer to personal consistency and an interior harmony within the individual. And they cannot be better identified than as the fruits of the Spirit that Paul enumerated in his letter to the Galatians (6:22-23): "love, joy, peace, patience, kindness, goodness, faithfulness, gentleness, and self-control."

THE THEOLOGICAL TRADITION OF PROPHECY

So far in considering the subject of moral decision making, I have examined first the ethical tradition of conscience that has formed the mainstream of Christian moral thought, and then what I called the quiet stream of spiritual reflection with its more placid religious tradition of discernment. This stream has become a kind of tributary to moral theology within the more theological approach that characterizes much post-conciliar moral reflection. Now, by way of completion of my subject and of the way in which moral theology should be moving, I turn to what I call the powerful hidden stream that has been running silently underground for centuries, the theological tradition of prophecy. In commenting at the time on the Instruction issued in 1990 to the church's bishops by the Congregation for the Doctrine of Faith on "The Ecclesial Vocation of the Theologian," I expressed regret that the document had expounded its argument about the role of theologians in terms of the theology of magisterium rather than having developed it from the doctrine of prophecy. For the document explicitly though briefly recognized the vocation of the theologian in the church as one of the special graces distributed by the Spirit of truth among the faithful of every rank to enable God's People to exercise their prophetic function in the world.[19]

In this reference, the Congregation was alluding to the developments in Catholic thinking about prophecy in the last twenty years as a result of rediscovering the biblical and theological description of Christ's triple role as prophet, priest, and king, and of applying this threefold function to the baptized who exercise in their lives the prophetic, kingly, and priestly characteristics of Christ. When we speak of Christ as king, prophet, and priest, we are referring to his possession of authority over the whole of creation, to his being a witness to God's concern and love for all humankind, and to his offering the whole world to his Father in worship and adoration. And when we speak of each baptized Christian as sharing in, and continuing to express, these aspects of Christ's activity, we are exploring how Christians are royally commissioned to exercise authority and power over creation and in society; how they are sent to be prophetic witnesses of God's Word of creative love for all women and men; and how they are consecrated in Christ's own priesthood to gather up the whole of creation and society and their fruits, and to offer them with Christ in his sacrifice of thanksgiving and adoration to God our Creator and Father.

At the time of the Reformation, Calvin powerfully developed this theology of Christ as priest, prophet, and king, and at the same time pointed out that "the papists use these names too, but coldly and rather ineffectually, since they do not know what each of these titles contains."[20] That accusation could not be repeated today, although it could still be said that Catholics are only slowly beginning to appreciate what each of these titles contains with reference to the individual Christian and the implications of this theology of Christian prophecy for the moral behavior and decision making of individual Christians— their prophetic witness, in word and in deed, of God's loving and saving design for creation.

For this witness to happen and to be appreciated, we need to unravel the historical process by which the kingly, prophetic, and priestly features of Christian identity became gradually absorbed by the clergy for a variety of reasons, some of which were sociological, psychological, political, and economic. The gradual professionalization of the clergy, partly under the influence of the levitical priesthood of the Old Testament and reinforced by the introduction and enforcement of celibacy; the powerful personalities of many church leaders; the mass conversion of whole tribes and illiterate peoples; the need to develop church structures that would also serve as social structures staffed largely by a clerical civil service; and the development of Latin from the *lingua franca* of the Western Roman Empire to become the preserve of an educated elite—these and other factors led to a class division within the church between the professional ministers and the ordinary faithful, who became increasingly the passive recipients of the pastoral ministries of bishops and priests.

This development can be seen in the way in which the church's liturgy became a ritual for spectators, and also in the way in which decision making in and for the church developed into jurisdiction as defined and distributed among the clergy by the church's canon law. In terms of the prophetic role of Christ and his disciples, this process of absorption was to be seen in the way in which all Christian moral teaching became centralized in the bishops, and particularly in the bishop of Rome. Christian prophecy thus became identified with the church's magisterium, and found its culmination in the distinction introduced in the eighteenth century between the *ecclesia docens*, the teaching church, that is, the bishops and especially the pope, and the *ecclesia discens*, the learning church, that is, everyone else.

With the gradual rediscovery of the fundamental significance of baptism into Christ, however, and thus into his kingly, priestly, and prophetic roles, it became only a matter of time and theological reflection helped by the ecumenical movement before the status of the laity within the church began to be reexamined. And with that has come the whole painful process of trying to reverse and unravel the historical and ideological process by which the clergy had absorbed most of the baptismal responsibilities and birthright of Christ's faithful, so that what began as the whole church's share in the kingly, prophetic, and priestly activities of Christ became centralized and concentrated into the bishops' official role in the church of "teaching, sanctifying and ruling."

This interpretation of historical events, I suggest, provides a helpful theological context in which to throw light on major tensions within the Catholic church today, all of which, I need hardly add, have a moral dimension and are therefore of relevance to our subject. Controversies about authority, administrative decisions, and power sharing are in theological terms attempts to identify how far the kingship of Christ is a monopoly in the church and not a Christian prerogative to be shared and exercised by all. Arguments about priestly ordination, celibacy, the ministry of women, and presidency at the Eucharist are manifestations of the need to clarify how Christ's priesthood is to be shared by all the members of his body.

Disagreements over the church's moral teaching and the moral behavior of Christians in such areas as sexuality, bioethics, and social justice are also evidence of an underlying attempt to identify what is the prophetic contribution precisely of the laity to forming the mind of the church in these matters. This entire theological agenda is already sketched out in the Second Vatican Council's decree on *The Apostolate of the Laity*, when it explains that "Christ conferred on the Apostles and their successors the duty of teaching, sanctifying and ruling in his name and power. But the laity, too, share in the priestly, prophetic and royal office of Christ, and therefore have their own role to play in the mission of the whole People of God in the Church and in the world."[21]

It is here that the principle of subsidiarity can be applied, and applied not simply in terms of jurisdictional decision making in the church, and not simply in terms of power sharing, but in terms of "power-recognizing" in the universal Christian exercise of the prophetic function of Christ. For what began as the whole church's prophetic role and subsequently became the episcopal and papal magisterium in moral matters, now needs to become the realization that all the baptized are commissioned by Christ to prophesy, that is, to give witness in all their moral decision making to human and Christian values in society and in the church.

There is always, to be sure, even in approaching moral decision making by way of a developed theology of prophecy, the danger of individuals deluding themselves and becoming, in the traditional phrase, "false prophets." But here the same important criteria apply that I have described within the spiritual tradition of discernment, with this added responsibility, that what is now under consideration is not just authenticating what one considers is God's influence on the heart of the individual as she or he considers moral decisions. What is now at stake is scrutinizing and validating the witness that God is calling one to offer to the church and the larger community.

CONCLUSION

We may be thought to have come a long way from my opening remarks about how we approach moral decision making, but I do not think we have lost our way. Rather, what I have been attempting to explore is the Christian way in which we may best understand and direct the moral enterprise and how, in the process, we may build up a cumulative understanding of what moral decision making entails for individuals as well as for the church of which they are privileged and responsible members. I began by exploring the philosophical and ethical manner of approaching such decision making in terms of conscience, a tradition that has flourished and developed in moral theology for centuries. I followed this by expanding the resources of moral reflection to include more explicitly theological considerations, including the whole spiritual tradition of discernment and the way in which the community and personal criteria that it offers may further enlighten our moral decision making as a response to the stirrings of God within us. And I have concluded by attempting to bring to the same activity the christological and ecclesiological considerations that bring out even more the deep Christian resources that exist by the grace of Christ within each baptized individual. These resources make of moral decision making not just the individual's wrestling with personal moral dilemmas or quandaries, but the offering of prophetic witness to society and the church of the values of the kingdom of God to which Christ himself gave witness and continues to witness through and in his followers.

Perhaps what I have offered for consideration can be summed up by expressing the responsibility of moral decision making at the ethical level in terms of the principle and maxim to "form and follow your conscience"; at the spiritual level in terms of the maxim to "know yourself and discern the spirits"; and at the theological, christological, and ecclesial levels in terms of the ringing appeal of Pope Leo the Great to the disciples in his day, "O christiane, agnosce dignitatem tuam": Christian, recognize your dignity![22]

NOTES

1. John Mahoney, *The Making of Moral Theology: A Study of the Roman Catholic Tradition* (Oxford: Clarendon Press, 1987), 184-193.

2. St. Thomas Aquinas, *De veritate* 17,3; Mahoney, *The Making of Moral Theology*, 191-192.

3. See *The Making of Moral Theology*, 196.

4. Second Vatican Council, *Decree on the Church in the Modern World*, 16. See *Decrees of the Ecumenical Councils*, Vol. 2, Norman P. Tanner, S.J., ed. (London: Sheed and Ward; Washington, D.C.: Georgetown University Press, 1990), 1078. My translation.

5. See *The Making of Moral Theology*, 270-271.

6. Paul VI, *Humanae vitae*, 4, *Acta Apostolicae Sedis* 60(1968): 487. My translation.

7. Ibid., 4.

8. Vatican II, *Decree on the Church*, 8.

9. Vatican II, *Decree on the Church in the Modern World*, 16; see *The Making of Moral Theology*, 292, n. 88.

10. R. Aubert, *La théologie catholique au milieu du XXe siècle* (Paris 1954), 76. My translation.

11. "*Tantum malorum potuit suadere religio.*" Lucretius, *De rerum natura*, Loeb Classical Library (London: Heinemann; New York: Putnam, 1924) i,76.

12. R.A. Knox, *Enthusiasm: A Chapter in the History of Religion* (Oxford Clarendon Press, 1950).

13. Aquinas, *Summa Theoligiae* II.II.88.a2.ad2. "In vovendo fuit stultus, quia discretionem non adhibuit, et in reddendo impius." The sentence is not in Jerome's extant writings, but see Peter Comestor, *Historia Scholastica*, Migne, *PL* 198, col. 1284.

14. Karl Rahner, *The Dynamic Element in the Church* (London: Herder and Herder, 1964), 73-74.

15. Yves Congar, "Pneumatology Today," *American Ecclesiastical Review* 167 (1973): 435-449.

16. Vatican II, *Decree on the Church*, 15: Tanner, vol. 2, 860-861; *Decree on Ecumenism*, 4: Tanner, vol. 2, 912.

17. M.C. D'Arcy, *Facing the Truth* (London 1969), 11-12.

18. *The Dynamic Element in the Church*, 104.

19. John Mahoney, "The Ecclesial Vocation of the Theologian: Some Theological Reflections," *The Month* 23 (8 August 1990): 304.

20. Calvin, *Institutes of the Christian Religion*, bk. 2, chap. 15, 1.

21. Vatican II, *Decree on the Apostolate of the Laity*, no. 2: Tanner, vol. 2, 982.

22. Pope Leo the Great, *Sermo XXI, In Nativitate Domini I*, 3; Migne *PL*, 54, col. 192.

7

Conscience

My subject is individual conscience. Each of us is taught to "let your conscience be your guide," but little is said about *what* conscience is or *how* to follow your conscience. Through what psychological processes does an individual conscience operate?[1]

Perhaps we can begin by saying what conscience is not and how it does not function. Conscience is not Jiminy Cricket or a guardian angel on one's shoulder or the voice of a little man inside a person. Conscience is not an isolated pang of feeling (such as a stab of guilt) or the passing memory of a maxim or commandment wafting through the mind. In fact, conscience is not a static "it" at all, but rather a human activity, a developed predisposition for activity of a special kind.

I prefer to define conscience as a personal, self-conscious activity that integrates reason, intuition, emotion, and will in self-committed decisions about right and wrong, good and evil. Mature human beings while alive and awake are always actively making decisions; but the decision making of conscience is devoted to moral standards of worth, or to responding to some ethical pull or demand.[2] Moral decisions and moral grounds for deciding are different from other standards based on efficiency, power, desire, aesthetics, custom, etiquette, or some combination of these.[3] The unique, personal, moral decision making of conscience concerns the right and good thing to do or the least evil thing to do, given a certain set of circumstances.

THE SCOPE OF CONSCIENCE

The scope of self-committed moral decision making is broad. We are not confined to the domain of what some have called "judicial conscience," making retrospective moral decisions about past behaviors.[4] We also engage in acts of "legislative conscience," deciding what we ought to do now and in the future. And these decisions can range from decisions about the next moment's action to decisions concerning our life's work. Conscience can govern small matters as well as large life and death decisions.

Nor is the engaged conscience confined to dealing solely with internal and external acts. (I should add that I consider human acts to include voluntary motor behavior, thinking, feeling, imagining, speaking, gesturing, and combinations of all the voluntary capacities that are part of the human repertoire.) We can also be morally committed to judgments about what others ought to do, or what ought to be the case in a particular set of circumstances (as, for instance, when functioning as a member of a family, neighborhood, political organization, church, or biotic community). The noted ethicist William Frankena has argued that, though we are individual moral agents, "we also wish to make judgments about what others should do. . . . We are also spectators, advisors, instructors, judges and critics."[5] We both vote our consciences and morally advise and instruct members of our professions or our families.

Personally committed decisions of conscience can be differentiated from other forms of moral thinking or ethical analyses. An intelligent person or a professional ethicist can engage in an ethical analysis of issues or review and weigh moral arguments, without taking a self-committed stand, much as one might size up the promises of a candidate for public office. But the tentative perusal of ethical or political options is different from the act of voting in the ballot box.

Personal conscience is engaged when the whole self—reason, emotion, and will—are integrated in moral decision making. Symbolically we speak of conscience as "the heart" of a human being, or even religiously as "the voice of God within."[6]

CONSCIENCE, CHARACTER, AND MORAL FAILURE

It is tempting to think that moral decision making presumes the kind of consciousness or attention one experiences when challenged.[7] But many, many actions, even moral decisions, are embedded in an almost automatic flow of habitual behavior and response learned in the past. Such behaviors, once learned—even if at the cost of great effort and attention—recede from consciousness.[8] Much of our moral behavior is the product of our past moral decision making as children within families or as socially participating members of our particular culture.

If we were asked why we do not knock down an old lady to get ahead of her in line, we would be able to explain that our conscience forbids such morally reprehensible behavior. But this particular moral commitment of conscience is so basic and so thoroughly learned so long ago, that it is now too habitual or automatic a part of our personality to command attention or count as a conscious decision. A limited fund of conscious attention is deployed upon deciding present challenging problems and troubling moral questions. Indeed, a person's moral development can be assessed partly by what options (or temptations) can hardly come up any more as a moral decision to be wrestled with in the ordinary course of the day.

Another indication of moral character is the level of behavior to which a person will not or would not ever sink, even in exceptional circumstances (such as life during totalitarian regimes, mass riots, or in concentration camps) when such a moral test may be severe.

Of course, when we look back over the course of our lives, we can see a series of changes in our moral insight and decisions of conscience. Some things that we once thought were morally acceptable we may now judge to be morally reprehensible. We can also remember with shame those times when we acted against our conscience and felt guilt.

Moral failure appears in various guises. One innocent form of failure, only judged retrospectively, springs from moral ignorance. Persons who live in a society that is generally ignorant of certain moral demands can hardly be blamed for following the moral conventions they were taught to follow, even when they seem morally reprehensible by other's lights.

For other moral failures persons may be culpable because they know in their core self what they are morally obliged to do, but, because of inner weakness or division, they give in to some insistent desire to attain a goal or to avoid pain, effort, or trouble. Conscience, or the core self's moral commitments, can be violated, overridden, or disregarded. Guilt and shame result from such self-betrayals. This inner guilt and shame can be experienced as ever-present and biting ("conscience" in Middle English was called "agenbite of inwit").[9] Such feelings are so painful and disturbing that they motivate action to restore personal integrity. Repentance, reparation, and change may be undertaken. Or, more ominously, painful self-judgments can stimulate psychological avoidance and flights into self-deception.[10] Self-deception is possible because, in the complicated ways that consciousness operates in micromoments over time, there are many chances to rationalize, turn away, distract, obscure, project, and disguise painful self-confrontations.

This complex self-deceptive semiknowing has been called "middle knowledge." As Albert Speer, Hitler's protégé said about his knowledge of the existence of death camps, "I did not investigate—for

I did not want to know what was happening."[11] Speer and others in similar situations can be held morally responsible for those momentary acts of voluntary turning away from the truth, when they know enough to know that their avoidance of perception of reality is motivated by their desire to deny a moral claim.

Other persons go further than defensive self-deception and consciously give up the moral quest altogether. They choose to become amoral, to be morally tone-deaf. Unlike people with mental disabilities or psychopaths, who may be morally impaired by some developmental or brain abnormality, intelligent, normally endowed persons can freely choose to abandon conscience or any standards of moral worth in their decisions. They may still adhere to social standards of achievement, efficiency, or even beauty, but moral concerns are meaningless to them. Their conscience has atrophied. The imperial self's pleasure, satisfaction, power, or comfort is the complete measure of all things. Such amoral people can be charming and successful and operate efficiently within the law to avoid trouble and ensure their personal safety. Their moral lacunae and selfish ruthlessness may be disguised except to their unfortunate families, intimates, and co-workers. They have "turned a deaf ear to conscience" so often that conscience becomes all but extinguished.

I also think there are persons who actively dedicate themselves to moral evil, much like Lucifer in *Paradise Lost* who says "Evil be thou my good."[12] Though their numbers may be few, these dramatic crusaders against all that others call good may be charismatic leaders, like Hitler, James Jones, or Charles Manson, who try to gain followers to wreak destruction and havoc in the cause of evil.

Nevertheless, most persons, I think, seek to be morally good, or at least good enough, and do not set out to be weak, self-deceived, or morally blind. For most people, conscience operates as a form of "generic self-guidance," or as "a sovereign monitor" of behavior.[13] When there is time to reflect, morally socialized persons will engage in moral decision making when some discrepancy or moral challenge arises.

THE OPERATION OF CONSCIENCE

A person can be challenged in conscience in at least two ways. One problem arises when one is already aware of what one is morally self-committed to do, yet experiences difficulty in deciding to act on the conviction. Another problem, which I wish to focus on here, is to decide what one should do or what ought to be the case, when challenged or confronted with some moral uncertainty. Of course, much depends on the nature of the decision and how much time a person has to decide. In emergencies one must act instantaneously and ordinarily behaves in accord with moral habits and capacities (or incapacities) arising from one's past life.

When there is time for moral deliberation and reflection and one does not turn away from the challenge, a complicated inner process can ensue. I see an adequate process of self-invested moral decision making to be anything but an orderly, linear, rationalistic, or deductive process of running through some decision tree or algorithm. The activity of conscience will more likely be a recursive, oscillating, interactive, dynamic process involving all of one's human capacities for reason, intuition, emotion, imagination, moving in many different directions. The focus of conscious activity is on the moral problem to be solved and on the self's moral integrity in the process of problem solving. When in good conscience one aims at a holistic, self-committed personal decision, who one is will matter, and especially how wholehearted one is in that quest.

I see a person's reason, intuition and emotions to be important resources mutually influencing each other in the complex decision making of conscience. I also think that moral deliberation and reflection involve mutual cross-checking and testing of all one's capacities and resources. One aims for congruence and fusion of reason, emotion, and intuition because the whole self is involved; no one way of knowing is infallible, though all are important.

Moral Reason

Those highly educated in professional disciplines and the sciences do not need to be persuaded to accept the value and power of reason. I, for one, am a grateful child of the Enlightenment and enthusiastically accept and endorse rationality and the scientific method as an articulated expression of our innate human capacity from infancy on to seek knowledge and understand reality. In the rational effort to know and avoid self-deception, we have developed common, public standards of rational judgment involving coherence, consistency, adequacy of evidence, and ecological validity. Science and other disciplines require reasoning to increase human knowledge in the modern world.

Refined methods of doubt, data collection, and skepticism operate to help us avoid bias and erroneous assumptions that occur from ignoring baseline data or the confounding of variables.[14] In reasonably accepting the probability of certain claims, we can point out to others the assumptions, principles, and data that justify our assent. I think moral reasoning and ethical analyses employ similar rational strategies and capacities. Moral knowledge can be rationally grounded; however, as in science, certain conclusions may carry different weights or vary in their probability levels of correctness.

Nevertheless, reasoning is not infallible outside of narrow logical deductions; the search for absolute certainty in either morality or science is doomed. High probabilities or virtual certainties are the best we can hope for in an open system existing like our real universe in ongoing time. Throughout history in the search for rational understanding, there have been paradigm shifts, evolutionary developments, and reconfigurations of knowledge and understanding. Human reasoning always operates within different frameworks and larger worldviews embodied in particular historical contexts and communities.[15]

Yet reason and common sense ensure that anyone who seeks knowledge must start within some community and group and build on what is already known. No one is self-made; no one can live and function alone, or invent either scientific or moral knowledge de novo. One turns to mentors and the practices of a community when seeking knowledge. Surely then it is rational for those seeking the morally good thing to do to turn to the wise and good members of their community. Those who believe in Christianity as God's word to humankind will turn for moral guidance to the church as the traditional community that has brought the good news and formed her members in the first place. Other papers in this volume address the complicated theological questions of how the moral guidance of the Roman Catholic church should be related to an individual believer's conscience. But all participants in the current intrachurch debates over the interpretation of tradition, authority, morality, and conscience argue for their views on rational grounds; and all agree that individuals who are believers must rationally accept their finitude and limitations by seeking moral guidance from their church community.

Intuition

The role of intuition in moral decision making, when not overlooked, is often devalued. Intuitions can often be identified as the ideas and thoughts that spontaneously come into consciousness without the effort of focused, directed thinking.[16] Correct intuitions are puzzling phenomena. The mythic concept of the Muses (goddesses of creativity and inspiration) was an attempt to understand how intuitions and innovative creative ideas come into consciousness. Psychology in various research enterprises tries to understand how these ideas and thoughts emerge.

Current scientific interest in nonconscious cognitive activity is high.[17] Research on implicit memory, implicit learning, nonconscious reasoning, and information processing points to the human mind's incredible complexity. It may well be that whatever one pays attention to in the present enters long-term memory, which then acts as a filter for future processes of conscious awareness and information sorting. At the same time, even more puzzling processes of dynamic nonconscious reorganizations of material in memory may produce the intuitive insights or creative solutions to problems that spontaneously emerge.

Mathematician Roger Penrose describes his intuitive scientific discoveries in which the solution to a problem he is wrestling with suddenly emerges while he is doing something else.[18] Other scientists speak of "building intuition" by working on a problem and then leaving the question alone to "incubate" for a time, in hope of an intuitive breakthrough. Penrose also claims that his own new ideas or intuitions come with different degrees of confidence; sometimes he is certain of the validity of his solution. While a good scientist must guess well and test rigorously, Penrose is sometimes convinced beforehand that the testing will prove the new intuitive solution to be correct.

In the moral life, our intuitions are also important. But we also must be skeptical, because our intuitions may prove to be incorrect—despite a felt sense of certainty. Moral intuitions must be rationally tested and grounded if they are to be convincing to others—or to ourselves. In a way, an intuition comes from a part of the mind that is inaccessible; it is a message to the self from the self. We should test our own intuitions the same way we would probe the intuition of another person. Whose intuition is it? How much does the person having the intuition know about the matter in question? How much has he or she wrestled with the problems involved? Einstein's intuitions about the universe, though not proven, are still taken very seriously because of his genius and because of his long work in his field.

Moral intuitions can be assessed in the same way. A wise and good person who has long wrestled with a particular moral problem will have a moral intuition that is worth more attention than the spontaneous opinion of a fool. What a person has attended to in the past and built into long-term memory will shape the intuitive flow of information into the stream of consciousness. The good news here is that we create ourselves minute by minute through voluntary acts of attention in the present and also shape our spontaneous intuitions for the future. Obviously, to have a developed conscience we must build into moral intuition ongoing acts of attention and moral concern.

Moral intuitions are a common resource of human conscience for everyone, but I think Christians actively seek intuitions when they pray for the Spirit's guidance when facing some moral challenge or dilemma. A believer turns attention to God and tries to listen for the divine will by discerning the value of any insights or thoughts that emerge into consciousness. Obviously, rational prudence is necessary for valid discernment as is evident in the long tradition in spiritual guidance dedicated to judging intuitions.

Emotions

Emotions have been the most neglected and devalued aspect of moral decision making throughout most of the Western tradition. Kant thought emotion was like a madness, a sickness to be cured before one could make a moral decision. In the Stoic tradition, emotions were suspect because they belong to the animal-like body—soon to be a corpse—that imprisons the soul. Emotions were also identified as feminine and, therefore, doubly suspect as irrational and of a lower order. Within much Christian thinking a negative view toward emotion crept in, so that complete emotional detachment was held up as the ideal state in which to make a moral decision.

Today, it is becoming clear that the traditional bias against "being emotional" (that is, wrong) arises through an inadequate understanding of human emotions. For one thing, the focus has too often been solely upon negative, regressed, childlike, extreme emotions such as rage, lust, and fear. The important role of positive emotions such as love, interest, and joy has been ignored.

The last twenty years have seen an explosion of research on emotion in psychology, partly as one of the by-products of psychology's cognitive revolution.[19] Once human thinking and consciousness was rehabilitated as a field of study, it became clear that emotions govern much of conscious life. Today emotions and the emotional system are seen as an evolutionary development that provides the main motivation for human behavior, including intellectual and sociocultural behavior. Emotions are necessary and adaptive for human survival and social functioning.

It now appears that all humans everywhere come equipped with an innate species-programmed affective system that produces, for example, the same facial expressions of emotion in New Guinea as in New York. Emotions also have differentiated conscious feeling contents and neurological components. Universal basic emotions appear in human development, just as language develops in all human societies. There remains disagreement, however, over which emotions are basic. Many list joy, interest, anger, fear, sadness, disgust, contempt, shame, and guilt as primary; others add love. Arguments abound about how these emotions become associated with one another in development and are shaped by cultural conditioning, but there is little doubt about the important role emotions play in motivation, communication, social interaction, and health.

Thinking and feelings are interactive and often fused together in mental structures. One dynamic model for consciousness is that of a musical fugue in which cognitive elements and affective emotions rise and fall and constantly interact. The important point is that not only can thoughts trigger emotions, but emotions can also trigger thoughts. They may be stored in memory together, since research shows that people who are made to feel sad will think more negative thoughts. Conversely, people who are made to feel happy will produce more positive thoughts, memories, and positive predictions.

Emotions always signal self-investment and engaged motivation. Therefore, they are vital for the moral life in many different ways. As we see with psychopaths, a numbing or lack of appropriate emotions means a lack of moral commitment. Compassionate identification with others is a necessary condition for insight and action in accord with the moral point of view. Guilt and shame are important, but so are love, sympathy, empathy, interest, and joy. Love, or joyful interest with a tendency to approach and become attached, is particularly important to morality because we pay attention to and value what we love. Love of truth and the desire for the morally best solution to a dilemma will motivate us to persevere in critical thinking.

Love of others makes us want their respect and to identify with them. The desire for moral esteem and honor among members of our group is a powerful moral motivator. Gossip is maligned, but gossip is one way that moral standards are articulated and enforced in a social group. Group approbation is so important that if we are repudiated by our present group, we may have recourse to or imagine moral approval from some other group of witnesses who would support our behavior. William James talks of one higher group to which one may morally appeal—and one on which Christians have certainly counted—as the "cloud of witnesses," the kingdom.

Emotions often spontaneously appear in consciousness in the same way that intuitions do. They too may be filtered through our long-term memory, as well as being responses to present stimuli in the environment. Those things we have attended to and loved in the past build up our attachments, emotional repertoires, and habitual emotional responses. No wonder persons of good character and virtue have certain worthy emotional responses.

In some cases, we can also enact emotions voluntarily and manage to feel love or sympathy by an effort of attention. Moral decisions and conflicts of conscience are often suffused with our struggles with different emotions as well as with conflicting reasons and arguments.

Isolated emotions, then, though no more infallible guides to conscience than reason or intuition, are a vital resource for a person making a moral decision.

THE ART OF MAKING MORAL DECISIONS

When we consult our conscience, morally reflect, deliberate, or ponder some matter in our heart, we use many different strategies and resources. If we think of intelligence as mental self-governance, we can use directed and spontaneous thinking and feeling in complementary and critical ways. We can engage in cross-checking and mutual testing, knowing that different resources are useful. Like a general on a battlefield or a mother attending to many things at once, we can use reasoning critically to judge arguments and test intuitive thinking.[20] Reason can also judge and tutor emotions, impelling us to amplify, curb, or enact more rationally appropriate emotions. Today most schools of psychotherapy are attempting some form of rational reeducation of emotions.

The more controversial claim is that intuition supplements, engenders new ideas and also monitors, checks, and judges reasoning. Yet experts of all kinds use their built-up intuitions in decision making. They sense where to look for relevant facts; they have a feel for which arguments to pursue and whether arguments that look promising are going to hold water. Spontaneous intuitive ideas enter the flow of all thinking devoted to problem solving, and in turn, they are tested. Likewise, moral intuitions and intuitive thinking infuse moral reasoning.

Finally emotions can tutor reason, intuition, and other emotions. Our loves, aversions, sympathies, interests, and empathies trigger thoughts, intuitions, and reasoning processes. Emotions monitor or tutor both positively and negatively. Our sympathy and compassionate identification with others, for example, may make us reappraise some reasoned argument and rethink a heretofore settled moral principle, say that blacks or women are inferior, or that AIDS patients should be denied medical treatment, or that the unborn are not humanly valuable. Moreover, when we admire and love another with whom we morally disagree we are also impelled to think again; sometimes we are inspired to attempt to feel morally or to value others as our valued mentor does.

Negatively, emotional reactions of horror at some proposal may keep us from assenting to some strong logical argument—for instance, to a proposal to harvest organs from those in irreversible comas, or to sell babies, or to employ torture for a good cause. We can be emotionally and intuitively repelled, or pulled toward a different line of moral reasoning. Emotions can keep us resisting, or alternatively, make us pay more attention to the problem at hand and start to reappraise our moral stance.

In an even more subtle process, one emotion can tutor, monitor, or override another. Love can cast out fear; sympathy can banish disgust; righteous anger can dispel depression and hopelessness. Moreover, the intrinsic qualitative characteristics of some emotions speak to the heart; envy, jealousy, and hate are experienced as dreadful and degrading, while love, joy, and sympathy are felt as positive and expansive.

Certainly Christians should be open to the ways that God's love for them and their love for Christ can gradually transform their thinking and moral reasoning. The fruits of the Spirit include emotional responses such as charity, joy, kindness, and peace. When emotionally felt, these emotions help produce thinking that engenders the more cognitive gifts of the Spirit such as counsel, knowledge, understanding, wisdom, truth, and piety. Enlarging the heart frees the mind; love for others and a love of goodness and truth keeps a person seeking, questing, paying attention, and engaging in a self-critical readiness to be corrected, changed, and enlightened.

In sum, I see the moral decision making of a conscience to be a dynamic, recursive, oscillating engagement between strategies and resources. As we reason, we may get certain intuitions, feel certain emotional pulls or aversions, which we then check and test. We seek information, guidance, and consultation with the wise and good and within our traditional community. Back and forth, in and out we go, round and round. We may imagine not only future consequences but emphatically imagine what we and others will feel if we choose a certain course. The mother, for instance, who shrinks from having her baby hurt by a polio injection steels herself when she imagines how she would feel if her child were to suffer from polio as a result of her aversion. Reason judges feeling, feelings, and intuitions assess reasoning. Spontaneous or enacted emotions tutor emotions. We may wait upon intuitions or seek an intuitive sense of rightness and appropriateness in our arguments and feelings. All our capacities, dimensions, or subselves are plumbed and engaged in coming to a personal, wholehearted moral commitment.

DECISION

At last we make a decision of conscience; our conscience is convinced
or settled. There is a difference between before and after. When the
mystery of a free human decision is examined, it seems to consist of
energy or emotional self-investment that charges the thought processes
with personal commitment.[21] Sometimes the decision process is prolonged; at other times, it is brief. Sometimes the process is fairly calm
and easy, sometimes turbulent and full of suffering. Williams James
spoke of some personal decisions as much like the murder of some
part or potential self that the decision cuts off forever. When external
forces and persecution are involved, a decision of conscience may actually be a matter of life and death; it may at least bring on great suffering or prolonged incarceration as a prisoner of conscience.

The engaged, fully adequate moral decision of conscience which
uses all one's personal resources can be imagined as like many threads
coming together and binding themselves into a strong rope. Other
images of integrating disparate parts can also serve: a whole gestalt or
picture emerges from the various parts; a chorus is made up of many
voices; a hologram takes shape from many different images. The more
adequate and thoroughly engaged the inner and external quest has
been, the more wholehearted the inner core self's commitment—and
the more immovable. St. Joan of Arc affirmed her love of the church
over and over, but she was also burned because she maintained, "And
what I have affirmed at my trial that I did at God's bidding, it would
have been impossible for me to otherwise. . . . Our Lord first served."
No wonder that so many persons have died and suffered for conscience's sake and that the persistent teaching of the church has been
that a person *must* follow one's conscience, erroneous though it may be.

CONCLUDING THOUGHTS

In this quick march through the intellectual terrain of conscience I have
skirted many deep, controversial problems and have had to leave
many questions untouched. One concern that immediately arrives is
how a person in good conscience can be committed to a decision and
yet remain humbly open to change, correction, or growth in the future.
Other problems involve those occasions when one is forced to act
while still struggling with inner conflicts, when one's conscience is
unsettled or unconvinced. Which resources and capacities are given
precedence when there is a lack of inner integration, conviction, or
wholeheartedness? Finally there remains the huge question of nurtur-
ing the growth of conscience in the young and in the mature. Once one

gives up a one-sided rationalistic deductive model of moral decision making, one must explore ways to enlarge the heart, educate emotions, and build moral intuitions—as well as encourage moral reasoning and hand on the moral principles and the moral truths of traditional communities. It becomes clear that moral decision making and moral development is a complex, holistic project that must focus inward on the self as well as outward on challenges from the world.

The worst thing that can happen, individually and collectively, would be to harden our hearts or have our consciousness become corrupt. Far better to engage in a conscience curriculum that goes on forever, fueled by a desire to be clear thinking and good hearted.

NOTES

1. For a comprehensive discussion and documentation of the ideas in this essay, see Sidney Callahan, *In Good Conscience: Reason and Emotion in Moral Decision Making* (San Francisco: Harper Collins, 1991). For a summary of Catholic moral teaching on conscience, see Joseph V. Dolan, S.J., "Conscience in the Catholic Theological Tradition," in *Conscience: Its Freedom and Limitations*, ed. William C. Bier, S.J. (New York: Fordham University Press, 1971). See also Timothy E. O'Connell, *Principles for a Catholic Morality* (San Francisco: Harper & Row, 1978), 83-97, and Richard M. Gula, S.S., *Reason Informed by Faith: Foundations of Catholic Morality* (Mahwah, New Jersey: Paulist Press, 1989), 136-151.

2. See Charles Taylor, *Human Agency and Language: Philosophical Papers 1* (Cambridge: Cambridge University Press, 1985), 97-114; see also Iris Murdoch, "The Idea of Perfection," *The Sovereignty of Good* (London: Routledge & Kegan Paul, Ark Edition, 1985), 1-45.

3. See William R. Frankena, *Ethics* 2d ed. (Englewood Cliffs, New Jersey: Prentice Hall, 1973); also, Thomas Nagel, *The View from Nowhere* (New York: Oxford University Press, 1986), 164-207.

4. Eric D'Arcy, *Conscience and Its Right to Freedom* (London: Sheed and Ward, 1961).

5. Frankena, *Ethics*, 12.

6. Walter E. Conn, *Conscience: Development and Self-Transcendence* (Birmingham, Alabama: Religious Education Press, 1981).

7. E. Roy John, "A Model of Consciousness," in *Consciousness and Self-Regulation Advances in Research* 1, ed. Gary E. Schwartz and David Shapiro (New York: Plenum Press, 1976), 1-50; see also Colin Martindale, *Cognition and Consciousness* (Homewood, Illinois: Dorsey Press, 1981).

8. Mihaly Csikszentmihalyi, *Flow: The Psychology of Optimal Experience* (New York: Harper & Row, 1990), 23-42.

9. See James Joyce, *A Portrait of the Artist as a Young Man* (New York: Penguin, 1964).

10. See Daniel Goleman, *Vital Lies, Simple Truths: The Psychology of Self-Deception* (New York: Simon and Schuster, 1985).

11. Quoted in Mike W. Martin, *Self-Deception and Morality* (Lawrence: University Press of Kansas, 1986), 38.

12. See Mary Midgley, *Wickedness: A Philosophical Essay* (London: Routledge & Kegan Paul, 1984).

13. Gordon Allport, *Becoming* (New Haven: Yale University Press, 1955), 68-74.

14. See Abraham Kaplan, *The Conduct of Inquiry: Methodology for Behavioral Science* (New York: Harper & Row, 1963).

15. See Alasdair MacIntyre, *Whose Justice? Which Rationality?* (Notre Dame, Indiana: University of Notre Dame Press, 1988).

16. See Kenneth S. Bowers, "On Being Unconsciously Influenced and Informed," in Kenneth S. Bowers and Donald Meichenbaum, *The Unconscious Reconsidered* (New York: John Wiley & Sons, 1984), 227-272.

17. See John F. Kihlstrom, "The Cognitive Unconscious," *Science* 18 (18 September 1987): 1445-1452.

18. Roger Penrose, *The Emperor's New Mind Concerning Computers, Minds, and the Laws of Physics* (New York: Oxford University Press, 1989); see also Michael Polanyi, *Personal Knowledge: Towards a Post-Critical Philosophy* (Chicago: University of Chicago Press, 1958), 18-32.

19. The literature on the psychology of emotion is extensive. A good summary of the field can be found in Carroll E. Izard, *The Psychology of Emotions* (New York: Plenum Press, 1991), and John G. Carlson and Elaine Hatfield, *Psychology of Emotion* (New York: Harcourt Brace Jovanovich, 1991).

20. R. M. Hare, *Moral Thinking: Its Levels, Method, and Point* (Oxford: Clarendon Press, 1981).

21. Paul Ricoeur, *Freedom and Nature* (Evanston: Northwestern University Press, 1966), 135-197; see also William James, *The Principles of Psychology* 2 (New York: Dover Publications, 1950 [1890]), 486-592.